Celestial Hemp

Celestial Hemp

Matthew Petchinsky

Celestial Hemp: Navigating the Zodiac Through the Green Cosmos

By: Matthew Petchinsky

Introduction: The Celestial Roots of Wellness

Since the dawn of human awareness, two ancient systems have guided our journey toward healing, wisdom, and alignment: the celestial patterns of the stars above and the botanical intelligence of the Earth below. *Astrology* and *hemp*—one cosmic, the other earthly—have traveled alongside humanity across millennia, whispering truths about our place in the universe and offering tools for balance, insight, and vitality.

Astrology, born of our ancestors' reverent gaze toward the heavens, became a universal language long before written alphabets. From the temples of ancient Egypt to the scrolls of Babylon, the night sky was not just decoration—it was *instruction*. Celestial bodies were seen as archetypes, storytellers, and timekeepers, charting the rhythms of personal fate and collective destiny. Every planet's orbit, every moon phase, was believed to echo in the human soul.

Hemp, meanwhile, quietly rooted itself in nearly every civilization as a sacred and utilitarian plant. Grown for fiber, food, and medicine, hemp was used in everything from ancient Ayurvedic healing to early American colonial agriculture. With its potent CBD compounds and minimal psychoactive effects, it provided relief for the body and calm for the mind. Hemp was not just a crop—it was a healer, a protector, and a symbol of sustainable living.

While astrology offered a cosmic blueprint, hemp grounded that blueprint into lived experience. Ancient traditions did not see these two systems as separate. The stars guided, the Earth responded. And through that relationship, we were meant to thrive.

This book invites you into a modern reawakening of that harmony. **Celestial Hemp** is more than a concept—it is a practice. It is the art of using hemp intentionally, aligned with the cosmic movements that shape your energy, your body, and your path. Every zodiac sign holds a specific vibration. Aries burns with forward motion; Taurus craves sensory pleasure; Gemini dances between thoughts. For each sign, there are *hemp strains, rituals, and remedies* that harmonize with their essence.

But this journey is deeper than matching plants to personality. It's about understanding the energetic weather of your life. Planetary transits, retrogrades, lunar phases—all of these create tides within you. And just as sailors read the stars before a voyage, so too can you prepare and align using Earth's natural medicine. A sativa-dominant strain for motivation under a waxing moon. A calming CBD tea during Mercury retrograde. A hemp-infused anointing oil for eclipse rituals. These are not just actions—they are alignments.

Through this book, you will:

- Discover the connection between your astrological profile and your body's wellness needs
- Learn how to use hemp to enhance focus, creativity, rest, sensuality, or emotional balance—based on your sign
- Explore rituals synchronized with moon phases and planetary movements
- Build a daily and seasonal hemp practice that honors both your birth chart and the living sky above you

You are not separate from the cosmos, nor from the soil. You are a bridge between them—a living ritual of breath, stardust, and green life. Let *Celestial Hemp* be your guide in remembering how to walk that path.

The stars will show you the pattern. The plant will show you the path.

Let's begin.

Chapter 1: Understanding the Zodiac

Decoding the Celestial Blueprint of the Self

The zodiac is far more than a tool for entertainment or a daily horoscope gimmick—it is an ancient, symbolic language that maps the inner architecture of the human experience. Rooted in thousands of years of observation and reflection, astrology has served as a timeless compass for navigating life's complexities. In this chapter, we'll explore the foundational structure of the zodiac, examining its twelve archetypes, elemental forces, and modalities. We'll also unveil the significance of the Sun, Moon, and Ascendant—the three cornerstones of your natal chart that reveal your personality, emotional dynamics, and public persona.

When we align our understanding of the zodiac with natural remedies like hemp, we create a holistic system for healing and self-realization that integrates the wisdom of the cosmos with the regenerative power of the Earth.

◈ The Twelve Zodiac Signs: Archetypes of the Soul

The zodiac is divided into **twelve signs**, each occupying 30 degrees of the 360-degree ecliptic—the apparent path the Sun takes through the sky each year. These signs correspond with constellations in the heavens and are associated with unique psychological, emotional, and behavioral traits. Each sign acts as a symbolic lens through which we can understand ourselves and others.

Sign	Dates	Symbol	Core Traits
Aries	March 21 – April 19	The Ram	Bold, energetic, independent, initiator, driven by action and passion
Taurus	April 20 – May 20	The Bull	Grounded, sensual, patient, values stability, comfort, and beauty
Gemini	May 21 – June 20	The Twins	Curious, adaptable, communicative, quick-witted, thrives on variety
Cancer	June 21 – July 22	The Crab	Nurturing, emotional, protective, deeply intuitive, connected to home and family

Sign	Dates	Symbol	Core Traits
Leo	July 23 – August 22	The Lion	Charismatic, expressive, confident, creative, thrives in leadership roles
Virgo	August 23 – September 22	The Maiden	Analytical, health-conscious, detail-oriented, devoted, practical
Libra	September 23 – October 22	The Scales	Diplomatic, graceful, fair-minded, seeks harmony in relationships
Scorpio	October 23 – November 21	The Scorpion	Intense, mysterious, transformative, emotionally profound, resilient
Sagittarius	November 22 – December 21	The Archer	Optimistic, adventurous, philosophical, truth-seeking, loves freedom

Sign	Dates	Symbol	Core Traits
Capricorn	December 22 – January 19	The Goat	Ambitious, disciplined, strategic, strives for mastery and legacy
Aquarius	January 20 – February 18	The Water Bearer	Innovative, eccentric, humanitarian, future-oriented, values uniqueness
Pisces	February 19 – March 20	The Fish	Empathic, dreamy, artistic, spiritual, deeply connected to emotional realms

Each of these twelve signs carries an energetic signature—a psychological and emotional archetype—that contributes to a person's total astrological blueprint. These signs form the basis for interpreting personality traits, relationship dynamics, vocational strengths, and emotional tendencies.

◈ Elements and Modalities: The Architecture of Energy

To understand how these twelve signs function in a broader context, we organize them into **four elements** and **three modalities**. These classifications provide further depth and nuance, helping us understand not just what the signs are, but *how* they operate.

◈ The Four Elements: Foundations of Expression

Each element represents a primary life force—an energetic essence that fuels the way a sign interacts with the world.

- **Fire (Aries, Leo, Sagittarius)**: Associated with passion, vitality, and inspiration. Fire signs are dynamic, future-focused, and action-oriented.
- **Earth (Taurus, Virgo, Capricorn)**: Grounded, practical, and reliable. Earth signs prioritize stability, material security, and physical well-being.
- **Air (Gemini, Libra, Aquarius)**: Intellectual, communicative, and idea-driven. Air signs focus on thought, dialogue, and social connection.
- **Water (Cancer, Scorpio, Pisces)**: Deeply emotional, intuitive, and sensitive. Water signs are guided by empathy, memory, and inner experience.

◈ The Three Modalities: Modes of Operation

Each element contains three signs, further categorized by **modality**, which describes a sign's method of initiating, sustaining, or adapting energy.

- **Cardinal (Aries, Cancer, Libra, Capricorn)**: Leaders and initiators. Cardinal signs set plans into motion and create momentum.
- **Fixed (Taurus, Leo, Scorpio, Aquarius)**: Stabilizers and preservers. Fixed signs build, maintain, and deepen structures.
- **Mutable (Gemini, Virgo, Sagittarius, Pisces)**: Adapters and transformers. Mutable signs are flexible, curious, and responsive to change.

The combination of **element + modality** creates the energetic signature of each sign. For example, Leo is a *Fixed Fire* sign—meaning it sustains fire energy through consistent creativity and leadership—while Pisces is a *Mutable Water* sign, capable of transforming emotional experiences and flowing between realities.

The Astrological Trinity: Sun, Moon, and Ascendant

While the twelve signs are universally recognized, the true depth of a person's astrological makeup is captured in what astrologers call the **"Big Three"**:

◈ **Sun Sign – The Core Identity**

Your **Sun sign** represents the essence of who you are. It symbolizes your conscious mind, your drive, your will to live, and the light you offer to the world. Often referred to as your "ego," the Sun sign is the central force of your personality—what you are growing into over time.

- Think of the Sun as your *central engine*—it powers your life purpose, your creative force, and your personal growth.

◈ **Moon Sign – The Inner Self**

Your **Moon sign** governs your emotional life, instincts, and subconscious mind. It reveals how you process feelings, nurture others, and seek comfort and safety. It often speaks louder in private life than in public roles.

- The Moon is your *emotional compass*—how you care, react, and self-soothe.

◈ **Ascendant (Rising Sign) – The External Self**

Your **Ascendant**, or **Rising sign**, is the zodiac sign that was rising on the eastern horizon at the exact moment of your birth. It shapes your outward personality, appearance, and the first impression you give to others. It also sets the tone for the entire layout of your birth chart, determining which signs rule the 12 astrological houses.

- The Ascendant is your *social mask*—how you move through the world and initiate experience.

◈ Integration: Why This Matters in Hemp-Based Healing

In the pages that follow, you'll see that knowing your **Sun**, **Moon**, and **Ascendant** offers a multidimensional understanding of your health, stress patterns, and healing style. For example:

- A **Capricorn Sun** may thrive on structure and long-term wellness plans.
- A **Cancer Moon** might need nurturing rituals and emotional calm through indica strains.
- An **Aquarius Rising** could benefit from futuristic hemp technologies and innovation in herbal self-care.

Understanding your full astrological identity allows you to **customize your hemp use** for optimal physical, emotional, and energetic harmony.

◈ Conclusion: Your Celestial Map Begins Here

The zodiac is not a rigid personality typing system—it's a symbolic language designed to help you navigate your life with greater awareness, alignment, and purpose. By learning the signs, elements, modalities, and core placements in your birth chart, you begin the journey of integration. And when that cosmic blueprint is paired with the ancient wisdom of hemp, the result is a healing path that honors both the stars and the soil.

Let's continue upward—and inward.

Chapter 2: Hemp 101

Understanding the Plant, Its Healing Powers, and Its Global Responsibility

Before we can align hemp with the zodiac, we must first understand what hemp is, how it functions in the body, and why it has become central to both modern wellness and sustainable innovation. This chapter provides a foundational education in the science, distinction, and ethics of hemp—a plant that has accompanied human civilization for thousands of years and is now reemerging as a vital ally in physical, emotional, and planetary healing.

◈ Hemp vs. Marijuana: Clearing the Confusion

Although hemp and marijuana are members of the same plant species—*Cannabis sativa*—they are not interchangeable. The primary difference lies in **chemical composition, usage, and legality.**

1. THC Content

- **Hemp** contains *0.3% or less* of tetrahydrocannabinol (THC), the psychoactive compound responsible for producing a "high."
- **Marijuana**, by contrast, contains significantly higher levels of THC—typically *5% to 30% or more*—and is cultivated for recreational or medical intoxication.

Thus, hemp **does not get you high** and is legally defined in many countries (including the U.S., under the 2018 Farm Bill) as a separate category from marijuana.

2. Usage and Purpose

- **Hemp** is cultivated for:
    - Industrial fiber (textiles, paper, construction materials)
    - Nutritional products (hemp seeds, protein)
    - Cannabinoid extraction (primarily CBD)
    - Sustainable bioplastics and fuel alternatives
- **Marijuana** is cultivated primarily for:
    - Recreational THC content
    - Medical cannabis prescriptions
    - Concentrates, edibles, and therapeutic products that include psychoactive components

3. Legality

- **Hemp** is legal in many countries provided its THC levels remain within the regulatory threshold.
- **Marijuana** remains highly regulated or illegal in many regions due to its psychoactive properties, although legalization efforts are gaining traction globally.

In summary, hemp is non-intoxicating, industrially useful, and legally distinct from marijuana. Understanding this distinction is critical as we explore hemp's role in personal wellness and planetary stewardship.

◈ The Health Benefits of CBD: Cannabidiol Explained

Among hemp's most powerful contributions to modern wellness is **CBD**, short for **cannabidiol**—a naturally occurring compound found in hemp flowers and leaves. Unlike THC, CBD is **non-psychoactive** and exerts its effects through the **endocannabinoid system (ECS)**, a vast signaling network that plays a central role in regulating internal balance.

◈ What Is the Endocannabinoid System?

The ECS is responsible for maintaining **homeostasis**, or biological balance, across several key functions:

- Mood regulation
- Sleep cycles
- Pain perception
- Immune function
- Appetite and digestion
- Stress and anxiety response

CBD interacts with **CB1 and CB2 receptors** in the ECS to support these regulatory functions, often enhancing the body's natural ability to self-correct and stabilize.

◈ Clinically Observed and Anecdotal Benefits of CBD

1. **Anxiety and Stress Relief**
   - Promotes a sense of calm and emotional equilibrium
   - Reduces cortisol levels and supports parasympathetic nervous system regulation
2. **Pain and Inflammation Management**
   - CBD has anti-inflammatory properties that assist with arthritis, injury recovery, and chronic pain
   - Works synergistically with other cannabinoids and terpenes in full-spectrum products
3. **Sleep Enhancement**
   - Aids with falling asleep and staying asleep by calming the nervous system
   - Helps those with insomnia or sleep disorders related to stress or chronic conditions
4. **Neuroprotection**
   - Preliminary studies suggest CBD may protect against cognitive decline, seizures, and neuroinflammation
   - Approved by the FDA for epilepsy treatment in rare pediatric conditions (e.g., Epidiolex)
5. **Digestive and Immune Support**
   - May alleviate symptoms of IBS, nausea, and autoimmune inflammation
   - Regulates gut-brain axis and promotes digestive calm
6. **Skin Health**
   - Antioxidant and anti-inflammatory properties benefit acne, eczema, and psoriasis
   - Topical formulations soothe irritation and support cellular regeneration

◈ Forms of CBD Delivery

- **Oils and tinctures** for sublingual use (fast-acting and customizable)
- **Capsules and softgels** for consistent daily dosing
- **Gummies and edibles** for gentle, longer-lasting relief
- **Topicals** for localized application to muscles, joints, or skin
- **Beverages and teas** as calming rituals
- **Vape products** for quick onset (not recommended for sensitive lungs)

Note: Always verify dosage, ingredient sourcing, and lab testing for any CBD product. Start low and increase gradually to assess your body's response.

◈ Sustainability and Ethical Consumption: Hemp for the Future

Beyond its therapeutic potential, hemp is emerging as one of the **most ecologically sustainable plants** on Earth. Cultivating and consuming hemp ethically is not only good for your health—it is a contribution to the planet's restoration and resilience.

◈ Environmental Sustainability

1. **Minimal Resource Requirements**
   - Hemp requires *50% less water* than cotton
   - Thrives without synthetic fertilizers or heavy pesticide use
   - Grows rapidly—up to 15 feet in 100 days—making it highly renewable
2. **Soil Regeneration**
   - Deep roots prevent erosion and detoxify polluted soils via **phytoremediation**
   - Leaves nutrients behind in the ground after harvest
3. **Carbon Sequestration**
   - One hectare of hemp absorbs 10 to 22 tons of CO_2 per growing season
   - Hemp materials in construction can *lock away carbon* for decades
4. **Zero-Waste Plant**
   - Every part of the hemp plant can be used: stalk (fiber), seed (protein/oil), flower (CBD), and roots (traditional medicine)

⟡ Ethical and Conscious Consumption

1. **Third-Party Lab Testing**
    - Choose hemp products verified for purity, potency, and contaminant-free status
    - Look for Certificates of Analysis (COAs)
2. **Transparent Sourcing**
    - Support brands that share farming locations, growing methods, and harvest cycles
    - Organic and regenerative farming practices are ideal
3. **Fair Labor Practices**
    - Ethical companies ensure safe conditions and fair wages for their workers
    - Avoid greenwashing by researching beyond marketing claims
4. **Packaging and Production**
    - Opt for companies using biodegradable or recyclable materials
    - Minimize packaging waste when possible
5. **Supporting Local and Independent Farms**
    - Buying local not only reduces carbon footprint but supports the growth of small-scale regenerative agriculture

◈ Bridging Knowledge and Ritual

Understanding hemp's biological effects, industrial potential, and ethical implications allows us to approach it not just as a supplement, but as a sacred ally. In the context of this book, you will learn to align specific strains, formulations, and hemp-based rituals with your astrological profile, life seasons, and celestial transits.

By respecting both the science and the soul of the plant, we honor hemp not just as a tool for personal wellness, but as a symbol of holistic living—where healing, sustainability, and cosmic alignment go hand in hand.

Your body is a temple. Your chart is a map.

Hemp is the green thread that connects the two.

Let's begin the journey into the zodiac.

Chapter 3: Aries – The Fiery Pioneer
Fueling Drive, Courage, and Vitality with Hemp

◈ The Essence of Aries

Aries, the first sign of the zodiac, ushers in the astrological year with vigor, courage, and an indomitable spirit. Governed by **Mars**, the planet of action, Aries is synonymous with **initiation, motivation**, and **fearless leadership**. This cardinal fire sign burns bright with ambition and instinct—constantly seeking movement, challenge, and opportunity.

Those born under Aries (March 21 – April 19) are natural trailblazers. They are bold, energetic, and driven to act—often without hesitation. While this intensity is a powerful gift, it can also lead to burnout, impatience, or impulsivity. For Aries, **balance lies in harnessing their vitality without allowing it to become erratic or destructive**.

Hemp, particularly strains rich in energizing terpenes and cannabinoids like CBD, serves as a valuable ally for Aries. It offers a sustainable way to maintain physical momentum, recover from exertion, and anchor their enthusiasm into daily wellness rituals.

◈ Energizing Strains for Motivation and Drive

For Aries, energy is not optional—it is essential. But too much unchanneled fire can lead to restlessness or irritability. Aries benefit most from **sativa-dominant** and **hybrid hemp strains** that support sustained focus, clean motivation, and physical endurance without overstimulation.

◈ Recommended Strain Profiles for Aries

1. **Sativa-Dominant Hemp Strains**
   - Promote alertness, clarity, and creativity
   - Ideal for morning use or pre-workout stimulation
   - Support Aries' desire to "go, do, and conquer"
2. **CBD-Rich Uplifting Hybrids**
   - Balance high-energy effects with mental composure
   - Aid in stress reduction while preserving momentum
   - Helpful for midday recalibration without sedation
3. **Terpenes for Aries**
   - **Limonene:** Enhances mood and motivation
   - **Pinene:** Boosts mental clarity and memory retention
   - **Beta-caryophyllene:** Provides anti-inflammatory support for post-exertion recovery

◈ Ideal Product Types

- **CBD-infused tinctures** with energizing terpene blends for quick and easy dosing
- **Vape formulations** for rapid onset during early morning exercise
- **Edibles or capsules** with time-released CBD for extended activity periods
- **Hemp-enhanced protein powders** for post-workout muscle recovery

◈♂ Hemp in Fitness and Performance Optimization

Aries thrives on movement. Exercise is not just a recommendation—it is a lifestyle imperative. Whether weightlifting, running, martial arts, or HIIT sessions, physical exertion is a direct expression of Aries' Mars-ruled essence. Hemp offers both **pre- and post-workout benefits**, optimizing performance and accelerating recovery.

◈ Pre-Workout Hemp Rituals

- Use a **CBD + caffeine blend** 30 minutes before workouts to enhance focus and physical readiness
- Apply a **hemp-infused warming balm** to muscles and joints for improved circulation
- Consume a **sativa-leaning tincture** to align the body and mind before physical exertion

◈ Post-Workout Hemp Recovery

- Apply a **cooling topical CBD gel** to reduce inflammation and muscle soreness
- Use **CBD isolate or full-spectrum capsules** for systemic relaxation and cellular repair
- Take a **hemp-infused electrolyte drink** to replenish hydration and promote muscle recovery

◈ Fitness Integration for Aries

- Design hemp-supported **morning workout routines** to align with Aries' natural circadian peak
- Use **smart recovery protocols** to prevent injury due to over-training or excessive competitiveness
- Embrace **mind-body hybrid practices** (yoga with CBD, dynamic stretching with hemp balms) to balance the warrior's intensity with grounded intention

⬦ Morning Rituals for the Aries Archetype

Morning is sacred for Aries. It is the time of ignition—the moment when purpose, power, and progress collide. For this sign, building a **consistent, energizing, and focused morning ritual** supported by hemp can transform restlessness into structured momentum.

⬦ Suggested Hemp-Infused Morning Ritual for Aries

1. **Hydration + Hemp Boost**
   - Begin the day with a tall glass of water infused with **hemp extract and lemon** to awaken metabolism and cleanse the system.
2. **Dynamic Movement**
   - Engage in a 20-minute physical activity—HIIT, martial arts, or cardio—primed by a **CBD + green tea tincture** to improve oxygen flow and reduce muscular tension.
3. **Power Shower with Aromatherapeutic Hemp Soap**
   - Use **peppermint- or citrus-infused hemp body wash** to stimulate alertness and lift mood.
4. **CBD-Infused Breakfast or Smoothie**
   - Add **hemp seeds, protein powder, and adaptogens** to your morning smoothie to build stamina and regulate mood throughout the day.
5. **Planning + Purpose Alignment**
   - Journal or visualize your top 3 goals of the day while sipping a **CBD-vanilla matcha latte**, using that time to harness Aries' clarity and vision.

◈♂ Managing the Fire: Hemp for Emotional Equilibrium

While Aries excels at *doing*, it can sometimes struggle with *being*. The sign's intense nature may lead to overexertion, short temper, or emotional fatigue. Integrating hemp for **emotional recalibration** is essential for preventing burnout and enhancing Aries' ability to lead sustainably.

◈ Evening Practices

- Use a **hemp-infused Epsom salt bath** to release tension and soothe overstimulated muscles
- Diffuse **lavender and hemp essential oils** to calm the nervous system before bed
- Consume a **CBD + magnesium supplement** to promote deep sleep and parasympathetic recovery

◈ Conclusion: Hemp as the Warrior's Ally

For Aries, life is a quest, and every day is a new frontier. But even the strongest warriors must care for their armor and their spirit. Hemp offers Aries a way to **sustain motivation, enhance physical vitality, and find balance amid their constant pursuit of progress.**

By incorporating energizing hemp strains, intentional fitness support, and restorative rituals, Aries can elevate its innate courage with focus, resilience, and clarity. In doing so, the Fiery Pioneer becomes not just a force of action, but a beacon of aligned purpose—burning bright without burning out.

Chapter 4: Taurus – The Sensual Grounded
Rooting Into Peace, Pleasure, and Presence with Hemp

◈ The Essence of Taurus

Taurus, the second sign of the zodiac, embodies the **power of presence, earthly pleasure**, and **unshakable stability**. Ruled by **Venus**, the planet of beauty, sensuality, and value, Taurus is the zodiac's connoisseur of comfort. Steady, deliberate, and deeply rooted in the physical world, those born under this earth sign (April 20 – May 20) possess a natural affinity for nature, touch, scent, taste, and all things luxurious.

Taurus seeks peace—not just as an emotion, but as a lifestyle. While Aries lights the fire of action, Taurus tends the hearth, building security, cultivating pleasure, and grounding into the moment. However, this fixed earth sign can become overly attached to routine, comfort zones, or sensory indulgence. When unbalanced, Taurus may resist change, stagnate emotionally, or overconsume as a coping mechanism.

Hemp becomes a powerful ally for Taurus by **amplifying relaxation, deepening sensory experience, and nourishing the body**. Through indica-rich strains, decadent CBD edibles, aromatic rituals, and grounding skincare, Taurus can create a daily sanctuary that brings both serenity and strength.

◈ Indica-Rich Products for Indulgence and Peace

Taurus thrives in environments of calm, warmth, and sensual fulfillment. They are most aligned when their nervous system is grounded and their senses are delighted. **Indica-dominant hemp strains and CBD-forward products** are ideal for helping Taurus sink deeper into embodiment, restorative stillness, and sensory pleasure.

◈ Recommended Strain Profiles for Taurus

1. **Indica-Dominant Hemp Strains**
   - Ideal for winding down, enhancing body awareness, and promoting deep rest
   - Slow the overactive mind, supporting Taurus's desire for peace and self-containment
   - Best used in the evening, during self-care rituals, or when seeking emotional stillness
2. **CBD-Rich Relaxation Blends**
   - Provide anti-anxiety and anti-inflammatory benefits without cognitive fog
   - Ease muscular tension and emotional reactivity while encouraging comfort
   - Great for integrating into daily rituals: skincare, bathing, or bedtime routines
3. **Terpenes for Taurus**
   - **Linalool**: Calming, floral scent that soothes the nervous system
   - **Myrcene**: Sedative and muscle-relaxing, excellent for deep body relaxation
   - **Caryophyllene**: Anti-inflammatory and emotionally stabilizing, ideal for grounding

◈ Ideal Product Types

- **CBD-infused bath soaks or oils** for restorative evening rituals
- **Hemp flower with a high myrcene content** for tranquility and muscle relief
- **Full-spectrum CBD tinctures** paired with magnesium or melatonin for enhanced sleep
- **Hemp edibles or herbal teas** with chamomile, lavender, or cacao for indulgent calm

◈ **Aromatherapy, Edibles, and Skincare: A Taurus Sensory Toolkit**

For Taurus, **wellness is best achieved through pleasure**. This sign responds exceptionally well to rituals that stimulate the five senses—especially smell, taste, and touch. Hemp-based products allow Taurus to integrate healing into their everyday life through **slow beauty**, **intentional nourishment**, and **luxurious stillness**.

◈ **Aromatherapy with Hemp**

Scent is one of Taurus's most sensitive and healing pathways. Aromatherapy using **CBD-enhanced essential oils** creates a direct link between the nervous system and inner peace.

Suggestions:

- Diffuse **lavender + hemp oil** in the bedroom to create a sanctuary of calm
- Use **CBD-infused pulse point rollers** (lavender, ylang ylang, sandalwood) to trigger relaxation during stressful moments
- Burn **hemp-based incense** blended with rose or cedarwood during evening meditation or bath time

◈ Edibles for Nourishment and Indulgence

Taurus delights in flavor, texture, and the ritual of eating. Edibles offer a unique way to blend hemp's medicinal benefits with the culinary enjoyment Taurus craves.

Suggestions:

- **CBD-infused artisan chocolates or truffles** with rose or orange blossom
- **Hemp honey or jam** on fresh sourdough or granola
- **Gourmet CBD teas** with vanilla, mint, cinnamon, or cardamom
- **Hemp smoothies** blended with cacao, banana, nut butter, and adaptogens

These edible rituals are not only pleasurable but also **support digestion, calm the body, and promote emotional grounding**—key pillars of Taurus wellness.

◈ **Skincare for Touch and Restoration**

Taurus is deeply tactile and benefits tremendously from physical self-care. Skin rituals help connect Taurus to the body, release stored tension, and activate Venusian self-love.

Suggestions:

- **CBD body butter or massage oil** for self-massage, especially in the shoulders and neck
- **Hemp-infused facial serums** for hydration and skin clarity
- **Clay and hemp masks** with chamomile or calendula to purify while calming
- **Body brushing** followed by hemp lotion to activate circulation and sensory pleasure

These routines provide not only physical renewal but also the emotional satisfaction Taurus seeks in quiet, intimate moments.

◈ Creating Sacred Space: Taurus in the Temple of Daily Life

Taurus is most fulfilled when home becomes haven. Grounding the body and nervous system through **environmental curation** is central to their healing. Taurus benefits from transforming their living space into a **temple of serenity**—a place to retreat, recharge, and indulge the senses.

Hemp-Based Enhancements:

- **Hemp-wax candles** scented with jasmine, rose, or vetiver
- **Weighted hemp blankets** infused with lavender pouches for sleep rituals
- **Woven hemp throws, cushions, and fabrics** for textural comfort
- **CBD-infused air mists or linen sprays** for freshening bedrooms and relaxation spaces

Ritualizing the ordinary is a Taurus superpower—and hemp gives them a medium to elevate the mundane into the sacred.

◈ Integration and Healing for Taurus

Taurus can sometimes become overly attached to what is safe, familiar, or comfortable. Hemp helps Taurus **soften emotional rigidity**, release physical stagnation, and connect more fully to the **fluid nature of life**—without surrendering their core need for security and peace.

◈ Practices to Deepen Grounding with Hemp

- **Evening yin yoga with CBD balm** for the spine and legs
- **Silent tea meditations** using hemp and adaptogenic herbs
- **Tactile journaling**—writing after massaging the hands with a hemp balm to access deeper emotional honesty

These practices create space for Taurus to access their full strength—not just through resistance, but through relaxation.

◈ Conclusion: Hemp as the Root of Sensual Strength

Taurus teaches us that healing is not always forceful—it can be slow, sensual, and deeply restorative. Through intentional use of **indica-rich hemp**, **aromatic therapy**, and **embodied skincare**, Taurus cultivates a grounded, luxurious life filled with beauty, pleasure, and peace.

Hemp is not a stimulant for Taurus; it is a *soil*—a place to root, recharge, and rise in stillness. By aligning hemp rituals with their elemental nature, Taurus learns that the deepest power often comes not from motion, but from the grounded choice *not* to move too quickly.

Chapter 5: Gemini – The Communicative Adapter

Harnessing Hemp for Mental Agility, Expression, and Social Harmony

◈ The Essence of Gemini

Ruled by **Mercury**, the planet of communication, intellect, and movement, Gemini is the zodiac's master of connection. Born between May 21 and June 20, Gemini represents the **air element in its most agile, inquisitive, and mutable form**. Often symbolized by the Twins, Gemini is known for duality of thought, love of variety, and a rapid-fire approach to both learning and expression.

Curious, witty, and mentally restless, Gemini thrives on new information, social engagement, and adaptability. These individuals are natural communicators—writers, teachers, conversationalists, and idea synthesizers. But their gift for mental agility can come with challenges: **overthinking, anxiety, scattered focus, and emotional inconsistency.**

For Gemini, hemp offers a balancing bridge—enhancing clarity while calming mental overstimulation. It empowers them to **communicate clearly, adapt to changing environments, and regulate their nervous system**. With the right strains and delivery formats, hemp can become Gemini's ally for both intellectual expansion and emotional steadiness.

◈ Hemp for Mental Clarity and Adaptability

Gemini's mind is a high-speed processor, constantly absorbing, analyzing, and broadcasting information. While this brings brilliance, it can also lead to **mental fatigue, nervous energy, and difficulty maintaining consistent focus**. Hemp—especially CBD-forward strains—supports **cognitive calm, emotional regulation, and flexible thinking**, enabling Gemini to channel their brilliance with greater ease and purpose.

◈ Recommended Strain Profiles for Gemini

1. **Balanced Hybrid Hemp Strains**
   - Combine the uplift of sativa with the grounding of indica
   - Perfect for Gemini's dual nature, supporting both alertness and calm
   - Useful during work hours, writing sessions, or social engagement
2. **Sativa-Leaning CBD Strains**
   - Stimulate creativity and mental alertness without overstimulation
   - Encourage curiosity and problem-solving
   - Ideal for brainstorming, studying, or multitasking environments
3. **Terpenes for Gemini**
   - **Pinene**: Promotes mental clarity, reduces memory fog
   - **Limonene**: Elevates mood and reduces social anxiety
   - **Terpinolene**: Supports creative thinking and gentle stimulation without jitteriness

◈ Ideal Product Types for Gemini

- **CBD tinctures or sprays** for on-demand clarity and calm during fast-paced days
- **Vape pens** with terpene-rich blends for rapid onset before public speaking or content creation
- **Hemp-infused nootropics** paired with ginkgo, bacopa, or lion's mane for cognitive optimization
- **Softgels or sublingual tablets** for extended mental stability during long creative sessions

◈ Hemp Use for Mental Balance

- Microdosing during the day can help Gemini **slow down racing thoughts** without dulling their intellectual edge
- Regular use can **reduce stress-induced distractions**, allowing for more deliberate and focused communication
- Pre-writing or pre-speaking rituals involving hemp can **enhance fluency, presence, and poise**

◈ Beverages and Social Strain Use: Gemini in Their Element

As a mutable air sign, Gemini is inherently **social, curious, and expressive**. They are often the center of conversation, fluent in humor, storytelling, and quick-witted banter. Hemp beverages and social-friendly strains help Gemini stay engaged, reduce performance anxiety, and avoid energy crashes during extended interaction.

◈ Hemp Beverages for Conversation and Creativity

Gemini delights in experimentation and convenience. Hemp-infused beverages offer a playful, easy, and socially acceptable way to incorporate cannabinoids into casual settings.

Suggestions:

- **Sparkling hemp tonics** with citrus, berry, or mint—ideal for summer parties or creative work sprints
- **CBD coffee blends** with adaptogens for early-morning inspiration or afternoon refreshers
- **Hemp lattes** with matcha or turmeric for heart-opening conversations and mood regulation
- **Cold-brew teas** infused with hemp and herbs like ginseng or tulsi to enhance clarity and stamina

These options are especially valuable for Geminis who experience **social anxiety masked by extroversion**, offering a smoother flow in high-energy environments.

◈ Social Strains for Engagement and Expression

Some Geminis may feel overwhelmed by intense group dynamics or underwhelmed by monotonous social routines. The right hemp strain allows them to **remain mentally agile and emotionally connected**, enhancing their interpersonal flow without mental fatigue.

Recommended Social Use Cases:

- **Before public speaking or live streaming**: Use a **CBD vape pen** with limonene-rich extract to open the throat and center the mind
- **During casual social events**: A **low-THC, high-CBD flower or pre-roll** can bring mental focus and openness without intoxication
- **At creative workshops or networking events**: **CBD gummies or chocolates** encourage comfort, adaptability, and clarity in connection
- **For virtual communication or content creation**: Hemp tinctures paired with ashwagandha or rhodiola can balance performance and endurance

◈ Gemini's Daily Hemp Rituals for Mind-Body Harmony

To harness their gifts without becoming mentally fragmented, Geminis benefit from **grounded morning rituals and centering evening practices**. These help reinforce focus, regulate nervous energy, and strengthen emotional follow-through.

◈ Morning Ritual for Focused Curiosity

- **Hydrate with a hemp-infused green juice** (spinach, apple, lemon, ginger)
- Take a **CBD + lion's mane tincture** to enhance neural plasticity and curiosity
- Practice **journaling or mind-mapping** with focus music and a pinene-rich vape nearby
- Use a **CBD topical balm** on the temples and neck to relieve tension from mental overstimulation

◈ Evening Ritual for Calming the Mind

- Unplug from digital devices an hour before bed
- Drink a **chamomile-lavender hemp tea** to quiet internal dialogue
- Bathe with **CBD bath salts infused with bergamot and cedarwood**
- Listen to binaural beats while applying a **hemp oil serum** to the skin, anchoring the sensory body

◈ Navigating Overthinking and Nervous Energy

Gemini's shadow emerges when the mind becomes **unmoored from the body**. Excessive multitasking, shallow distraction, and nervous talking are symptoms of imbalance. Hemp helps **restore integration between intellect and intuition**, allowing Gemini to move from reaction to reflection.

Practices to Support Integration:

- **CBD-assisted breathwork or meditation** to slow racing thoughts
- **Grounding movement (walking, stretching, Tai Chi)** paired with social music and aromatherapy
- **Digital detox days** supported by **CBD tinctures and nature immersion**

◈ Conclusion: Hemp as the Airborne Anchor

For Gemini, life is a series of ideas, conversations, and constant evolution. But to truly thrive, this sign must learn not only to communicate—but to *pause*. Hemp provides Gemini with the tools to **think clearly, express authentically, and live lightly**—without sacrificing the brilliance of their active minds.

By integrating CBD for cognitive clarity, creative expression, and nervous system balance, Gemini becomes not just a messenger—but a mindful translator of universal ideas.

Chapter 6: Cancer – The Nurturing Protector

Harnessing Hemp for Emotional Security, Self-Care, and Inner Resilience

◈ The Essence of Cancer

Cancer, the fourth sign of the zodiac, is the archetype of the **nurturer, empath, and emotional protector**. Governed by the Moon—the celestial body that governs tides, rhythms, and emotions—Cancer is intimately connected to **intuition, home, memory, and emotional cycles**. Those born under Cancer (June 21 – July 22) are deeply sensitive, protective, and attuned to the emotional undercurrents of themselves and others.

Cancer is the caregiver of the zodiac. Their strength lies in creating sanctuary—for loved ones and for themselves. Yet their emotional attunement can also become their vulnerability. Overwhelm, emotional exhaustion, mood fluctuations, and a tendency to retreat into protective shells are common challenges. They often give more than they receive, absorbing emotional energy without always having the tools to release it.

Hemp, especially in calming, restorative forms, offers Cancer a sacred refuge. When used mindfully, it becomes a plant ally that soothes the nervous system, restores emotional equilibrium, and fortifies Cancer's intuitive gifts without depleting their reserves. Through **bath rituals, skincare, emotional self-care, and internal grounding**, hemp helps Cancer build boundaries and serenity from the inside out.

◈ Comforting Hemp for Emotional Well-Being

For Cancer, emotional security is non-negotiable. They thrive when they feel safe—physically, emotionally, and spiritually. Hemp supports Cancer's **emotional depth** by quieting mental overstimulation, easing nervous tension, and nurturing internal softness. It offers an anchor for those days when the world feels too loud or their empathy becomes overwhelming.

◈ Recommended Strain Profiles for Cancer

1. **Indica-Dominant CBD Strains**
   - Offer a calming, body-centered effect ideal for emotional decompression
   - Help Cancer retreat into restorative solitude after social or caregiving exertion
   - Perfect for use in evening rituals or moments of inner retreat

2. **CBD Isolates and Full-Spectrum Products**
   - Provide reliable relief from emotional spikes without psychoactive effects
   - Help regulate sleep, mood, and stress with gentle, sustained support
   - Particularly valuable for highly sensitive or empathic Cancers

3. **Terpenes for Cancer**
   - **Linalool**: Sedative, calming, and ideal for emotional rebalancing
   - **Myrcene**: Supports sleep, reduces tension, and soothes physical stress
   - **Bisabolol**: Anti-inflammatory and emotionally stabilizing, often found in chamomile and effective for skin and heart health

◈ Ideal Product Types for Cancer

- **CBD-infused herbal teas or tinctures** for calming the heart and digestive system
- **Topical oils and balms** for comfort and sensory connection
- **Sleep aids** with melatonin, magnesium, and CBD to support deep rest
- **Inhalable aromatherapy blends** using hemp oil, rose, and lavender for emotional reset

◈ Baths, Self-Care Rituals, and Emotional Defense

Cancer's natural habitat is the home—and specifically, the **sanctuary of the bathroom and bedroom**. These are sacred spaces where Cancer can **release, retreat, and restore**. Hemp-based self-care rituals reinforce the emotional boundaries they need to feel safe and centered.

◈ Bath Rituals for Energetic Release

Water is Cancer's elemental domain, making **baths an ideal setting** for emotional clearing and nervous system reset. Infusing this ritual with hemp elevates it into a holistic act of healing.

Suggested Hemp Bath Ritual:

1. **Create an emotional cocoon**: Dim the lights, light a hemp wax candle, and play soft music or lunar soundscapes.
2. **Use a CBD-infused Epsom salt soak** with lavender, rose, or chamomile to calm muscles and the emotional body.
3. **Add a few drops of hemp essential oil** (paired with jojoba or almond oil) to the water for aromatherapeutic benefits.
4. **Set an intention to release emotional weight**, speaking it aloud or journaling beforehand.
5. After soaking, wrap in a plush towel and apply a **CBD-rich body lotion** to lock in moisture and comfort.

This ritual not only soothes the physical body but **reclaims emotional space**—essential for Cancers who frequently overextend their energy toward others.

◈ Self-Care as Emotional Armor

For Cancer, self-care is not vanity—it is **emotional defense**. When Cancer takes time to honor their body and feelings, they strengthen the psychic shield they need to move through the world with clarity and protection.

Hemp-Infused Self-Care Ideas for Cancer:

- **CBD facial oils or masks** infused with rosehip or blue chamomile for calming and hydration
- **Hemp seed oil massage candles** used for touch therapy or massage with a trusted partner
- **Herbal CBD pillow sprays** for nighttime rituals and dreamwork
- **Journaling after hemp tea** to transmute complex emotions into clarity and release

These routines help Cancer stay **connected to their intuition** while maintaining healthy emotional boundaries—allowing them to love deeply without draining themselves.

◈♀ **Emotional Defense and Grounding Practices**

Cancer is an empathic sponge. They easily absorb emotional energy from others—especially from family or close relationships. To remain emotionally sovereign, they need daily practices that **shield their aura, clear residual energy, and root them into their own emotional truth**.

◈ **Hemp-Assisted Grounding for Cancer:**

- **Morning grounding ritual**: Place a few drops of CBD oil under the tongue and walk barefoot outside for 10 minutes. Speak a grounding affirmation such as, "I belong to myself. I nurture from a full cup."
- **Evening clearing spray**: Mix rose water, hemp extract, and a pinch of sea salt. Mist the body or room after social interactions to release attachments.
- **CBD-assisted visualization**: Inhale from a hemp diffuser and visualize a glowing shell of light around your heart and home.

These rituals reinforce Cancer's ability to give without depletion, love without self-sacrifice, and care without collapse.

◈ Creating a Hemp-Infused Sanctuary

More than any other sign, Cancer requires a **nurturing, energetically protective environment** to thrive. Turning the home into a sanctuary not only uplifts the spirit but serves as an emotional reset after being in the outside world.

Sanctuary-Building Tips for Cancer:

- Use **hemp textiles** (curtains, throws, or cushions) in soft colors like pearl, ocean blue, or silver
- Place **CBD diffuser blends** near entryways and bedrooms to protect energy flow
- Keep a **ritual basket** with hemp teas, journals, calming sprays, and crystal companions like moonstone or rose quartz
- Decorate bath areas with **water-safe plants**, candles, and hemp-infused beauty products to create a spa-like escape

Home is not just a place for Cancer—it's an **extension of their emotional body**. Hemp helps them maintain this space with intention, serenity, and sacred presence.

◈ Conclusion: Hemp as the Lunar Healer

Cancer's superpower is their heart—vast, sensitive, and nurturing. But even protectors need protection. Hemp serves as **Cancer's lunar ally**, offering comfort when emotions overflow, strength when boundaries blur, and stillness when the world feels too much.

By incorporating calming hemp rituals into daily life—through **baths, bodywork, beverages, and energetic clearing**—Cancer learns that **self-care is not a retreat from the world, but a return to the self**.

Chapter 7: Leo – The Radiant Creator
Empowering Creativity, Confidence, and Charisma with Hemp

◈ The Essence of Leo

Leo, the fifth sign of the zodiac, embodies the **sun's illuminating brilliance**—radiating confidence, joy, and artistic power. Governed by the **Sun**, Leo is the sign of **self-expression, leadership, play, and performance**. Those born between July 23 and August 22 are natural entertainers, creatives, and visionaries with a magnetic charm and an unshakable desire to leave their mark on the world.

Leos thrive in the spotlight, and their lives are often infused with theatrical flair, creativity, and big-hearted generosity. At their best, they are **inspirational leaders**, **courageous dreamers**, and **unapologetic artists**. However, when out of balance, Leo can become self-conscious, creatively blocked, or emotionally drained by external validation.

Hemp serves as a **sacred firelighter** for Leo's creative flame—supporting emotional relaxation, deepening imaginative flow, and anchoring the nervous system during high-performance periods. Whether through bold, focus-enhancing strains or calming rituals of self-appreciation, hemp can amplify Leo's radiance while protecting their inner vitality.

◈ Bold Strains for Creativity and Self-Expression

Leo is fueled by passion, inspiration, and the desire to create something meaningful. They are happiest when their internal fire finds outward expression—whether through music, storytelling, fashion, performance, or leadership. The right hemp can **spark the creative mind**, reduce performance anxiety, and sustain stamina during bursts of inspiration.

◈ Recommended Strain Profiles for Leo

1. **Sativa-Dominant Hemp Strains**
   - Stimulate creative thought and elevate mood
   - Perfect for brainstorming, content creation, artistic performance, and idea generation
   - Help Leo stay inspired while avoiding mental fatigue
2. **CBD Hybrid Strains for Flow States**
   - Maintain clarity and focus without overstimulation
   - Support emotional steadiness while engaging in public expression
   - Ideal for long studio sessions, workshops, or live performances
3. **Terpenes for Leo**
   - **Limonene**: Uplifting, promotes joy and confidence
   - **Pinene**: Enhances memory and mental clarity—great for memorization and storytelling
   - **Ocimene**: Stimulates alertness and sociability—enhancing Leo's natural charisma

◇ **Ideal Product Types**

- **CBD + terpene vape pens** for pre-performance boost
- **Hemp nootropic blends** with brain-enhancing herbs like rhodiola, ginseng, and lion's mane
- **CBD edibles with cacao or cinnamon** to match Leo's love of bold flavor and luxurious rituals
- **Fast-acting tinctures** for on-the-go creative sessions or stage prep

◈ Hemp for Performance, Relaxation, and Artistic Presence

As a sign of theatrical flair and emotional generosity, Leo often gives enormous energy to their craft and community. Whether they're performing onstage, painting at dawn, running a business, or guiding a team, Leo needs **rituals that recharge and restore their internal light**. Hemp offers versatile support for both **creative expansion and emotional replenishment**.

◈ Hemp for Performance Support

Performing, public speaking, and creating in high-stress settings can lead to **adrenal fatigue, creative burnout, or anxiety**—even for confident Leos. Strategic hemp use helps sustain the magic without draining the performer.

Suggestions for Leo's Performance Prep:

- Inhale a **limonene-rich vape** 20 minutes before a show or presentation to spark confidence
- Sip on a **CBD + matcha beverage** to energize and calm without jittery nerves
- Use **hemp salves on pressure points** (wrists, temples, chest) to ground the body before stepping into the spotlight
- Carry **CBD gum or mints** backstage for fast-acting calm between scenes or sets

◇ **Hemp for Artistic Rituals and Creative Flow**

Leo's creativity is sacred. It flows best when the heart is open, the body relaxed, and the mind uncluttered. Hemp becomes a bridge into the **flow state**—that timeless space where creation feels effortless and alive.

Creative Rituals for Leo:

- Create a "studio altar" with **hemp incense, sunflowers, crystals (like citrine or carnelian), and sketchbooks**
- Begin art sessions with **CBD tea** (lavender, vanilla, or orange peel) to open the senses
- Burn a **CBD candle** during long creative blocks to inspire momentum and imagination
- Journal freely after ingesting a **low-dose CBD gummy** to loosen perfectionism and ignite new ideas

◈ Leo's Self-Care: Restoring the Inner Flame

While Leo thrives on applause and impact, their **inner world** is often under-prioritized. The emotional vulnerability beneath Leo's confidence requires deep care. They must regularly unplug, rest, and **shine inward**. Hemp aids in these quieter moments by reinforcing **emotional resilience, body appreciation, and creative regeneration**.

◈ Morning Rituals

- Start with a **CBD tincture + citrus juice elixir** to awaken joy and motivation
- Meditate facing sunlight for 10 minutes, visualizing your inner flame being fueled by warmth
- Stretch or dance with music that honors Leo's solar nature
- Apply a **CBD body oil with golden mica or shimmer** to the heart, shoulders, and chest as an act of self-honoring

◈ Evening Wind-Down

- Take a **CBD-infused bath** with rose petals and gold candles to soothe overstimulated nerves
- Use a **hemp facial mask** while reflecting on the day's accomplishments—big or small
- Light a **hemp-scented candle** and read poetry, listen to jazz, or sketch in silence
- Practice **mirror affirmations** after applying CBD cream to the chest or solar plexus:
  "I am enough, even in stillness."

◈ The Heart of Leo: Emotional Courage and Hemp

Leo rules the heart—literally and symbolically. They are **romantics, givers, and protectors** who often mask their vulnerability behind a radiant exterior. Hemp helps Leo **remain open-hearted without becoming overextended**, softening emotional pride while honoring personal truth.

Hemp Practices for Emotional Bravery:

- Before difficult conversations: Take a **CBD + ashwagandha blend** to support calm expression
- After rejection or burnout: Soak in a **hemp + calendula bath** and journal the truth beneath the performance
- When craving validation: Light a **CBD candle**, breathe deeply, and ask: "What do I need to give *myself* right now?"

◈ Conclusion: Hemp as the Mirror and Muse

Leo reminds us that we are all worthy of shining—of expressing, creating, and being fully seen. But the brightest flames require fuel, care, and renewal. Hemp offers Leo not just enhancement, but **integration**—supporting performance, celebration, and quiet restoration in equal measure.

By aligning with bold hemp strains and mindful rituals, Leo transforms performance into presence and charisma into soul expression. In this alignment, the Radiant Creator becomes a living sun—burning with brilliance, love, and authenticity that heals everyone they touch.

Chapter 9: Libra – The Harmonious Balancer

Cultivating Connection, Aesthetic Flow, and Inner Equilibrium with Hemp

◇ The Essence of Libra

Libra, the seventh sign of the zodiac, stands as the sacred bridge between self and other. Ruled by **Venus**, the planet of love, beauty, and aesthetics, Libra governs **relationships, balance, justice, diplomacy, and artistry**. Those born between September 23 and October 22 are natural harmonizers—attuned to social cues, emotionally intelligent, and deeply invested in cultivating fairness and beauty in their surroundings.

Represented by the Scales, Libra seeks not neutrality, but **elegant equilibrium**—a graceful calibration of opposing forces. While gifted in charm, collaboration, and refined taste, Libra can also struggle with indecision, people-pleasing, and emotional disorientation in conflict. Their challenge is to find harmony without sacrificing authenticity.

Hemp offers Libra a holistic toolset: from **hybrid strains that support social poise**, to rituals that foster **emotional peace and aesthetic pleasure**. Whether mediating tension, curating a gathering, or expressing their creative vision, hemp allows Libra to stay present, diplomatic, and delightfully balanced.

◈ Hybrid Strains for Social Grace

Libra thrives in **connected environments**—gatherings, artistic salons, collaborative projects, and intimate conversations. But as natural empathic mirrors, they can absorb conflicting energies or become overwhelmed by decision-making. Hybrid hemp strains provide the **dual action** Libra needs: **uplifting and grounding, energizing and calming**—the botanical embodiment of balance.

◈ Recommended Strain Profiles for Libra

1. **Balanced Hybrids (CBD-rich, 1:1 or 2:1)**
   - Support both social engagement and emotional regulation
   - Prevent overstimulation or fatigue during events
   - Perfect for artistic collaborations or peaceful dialogue
2. **Low-THC Hemp with Uplifting Terpenes**
   - Allow Libra to stay mentally sharp and socially fluid
   - Minimize fogginess while promoting soft-hearted openness
3. **Terpenes for Libra**
   - **Linalool**: Soothes emotional conflict and promotes graceful communication
   - **Ocimene**: Enhances sociability and fresh thinking
   - **Geraniol**: Venusian in nature—floral, luxurious, emotionally harmonizing

⬦ Ideal Product Types for Libra

- **Vape pens with citrus + floral profiles** for pre-event or conflict-resolution settings
- **CBD mints or breath sprays** to freshen and calm before important social exchanges
- **Microdose tinctures** used during creative workshops or shared meals
- **Infused hemp aperitifs** for elegant, alcohol-free celebrations

◈ **Hemp During Gatherings, Connection, and Creative Flow**

Social life is Libra's creative canvas. From intimate dinner parties to curated community events, they intuitively create environments where others feel seen, heard, and valued. Hemp enhances this artistry by **relaxing anxiety, inspiring dialogue, and elevating ambiance**—without overpowering the subtle nuances Libra loves to cultivate.

◈ **Social Rituals with Hemp for Libra**

Before Hosting:

- Mist rooms with a **CBD-infused lavender + vanilla spray** to set a peaceful tone
- Brew a **CBD hibiscus rose tea** for centering elegance
- Apply a **hemp balm to hands and temples** for grounding before guests arrive

During Gatherings:

- Offer **sparkling hemp-based mocktails** with fresh herbs (basil, mint, orange peel)
- Provide **CBD chocolates or gummies** as luxurious favors
- Keep **low-dose vape pens or diffusers** in shared creative spaces for inspiration without intoxication

Post-Gathering Wind Down:

- Soak in a **rose and hemp oil bath** with calming music and moonlight
- Reflect on social interactions with gentle journaling, supported by a relaxing CBD tincture

These rituals allow Libra to **give socially without energetic depletion,** keeping their heart open and boundaries intact.

◈ Hemp as Muse: Aesthetic and Artistic Alignment

Libra possesses a refined aesthetic sensibility—whether in interior design, music, fashion, or the fine arts. Beauty is not surface to them; it is **soul-symmetry**. Hemp unlocks access to **creative zones of perception** by relaxing the inner critic and allowing flow without perfectionism.

Hemp-Fueled Artistic Rituals for Libra

- Inhale from a **hemp diffuser** before starting a painting, poem, or playlist
- Set a visual altar with **Venusian herbs** (rose, mugwort, blue lotus) and CBD tea
- Use a **CBD roll-on** infused with ylang-ylang or neroli when choosing colors or fabrics
- Collaborate on music, visual art, or writing while sipping **chilled CBD botanical blends**

By softening the ego and heightening sensory intuition, hemp helps Libra **make art that heals and invites harmony.**

◈ Conflict Resolution and Internal Balance

Despite their social fluency, Libra often **internalizes discord**. Confrontation and imbalance—whether external or internal—can deeply unsettle them. They may suppress their truth for the sake of peace, which leads to **emotional dissonance, resentment, or indecision**. Hemp supports Libra in **navigating conflict with calm clarity**, encouraging resolution without self-erasure.

◈ Conflict Recovery Toolkit (Hemp Edition)

- **CBD + passionflower tincture** to prepare for emotionally charged conversations
- **Journaling with hemp-infused aromatherapy** to clarify needs before speaking
- **Post-discussion hemp cacao ritual** to rebuild heart-centered connection
- **Evening self-massage** with CBD oil on the chest and throat chakra while reciting:

"My peace is rooted in truth. My voice restores balance."

By using hemp in conscious, reflective ways, Libra learns to **honor both sides of the scale—their needs and the needs of others**—with elegance and integrity.

◈ Libra's Sanctuary: Curating Calm Through Beauty

Home is not just shelter for Libra—it is a **mirror of inner peace**. Curated spaces, harmonious lighting, and elegant rituals calm their often overstimulated mind. Hemp assists in making home a temple of relaxation, refinement, and relational ease.

Design Tips for Libra's Hemp-Infused Home:

- Use **hemp textiles** in soft cream, blush, or powder blue for visual tranquility
- Set up a **CBD tea station** with floral blends and infused honey
- Display **infused soy candles or incense** in Venusian scents (ylang-ylang, sandalwood, rose)
- Keep a **conflict-resolution toolkit** (CBD roll-on, affirmation cards, herbal teas) in a visible place for emotional grounding

◈ Conclusion: Hemp as the Bridge Between Grace and Grounding

Libra walks the fine line between inner balance and outer beauty. Their brilliance lies not in denying conflict, but in resolving it with **compassion, clarity, and charm**. Hemp offers a perfect botanical partnership—anchoring Libra's airiness with calm focus, nourishing their aesthetic heart, and empowering honest, soulful communication.

In embracing hemp through social rituals, artistic expression, and relational healing, Libra becomes the embodiment of Venus: a **living vessel of harmony, grace, and elevated connection.**

Chapter 10: Scorpio – The Intense Transformer

Harnessing Hemp for Shadow Integration, Emotional Depth, and Personal Power

◈ The Essence of Scorpio

Scorpio, the eighth sign of the zodiac, is the sign of **transformation, intensity, power, and deep emotional truth**. Ruled traditionally by **Mars** and, in modern astrology, by **Pluto**, Scorpio governs the unseen realms—death and rebirth, trauma and healing, desire and transcendence. Those born between October 23 and November 21 are often mysterious, magnetic, and fiercely loyal, with a drive to understand life at its most profound levels.

Scorpio is not content with surface living. This sign dives into the undercurrents of emotion, psychology, and soul evolution. Scorpios are the natural alchemists of the zodiac: drawn to pain not to suffer, but to **transmute it**. But with such depth comes emotional volatility, intensity, and the risk of internalizing pain. Hemp offers Scorpio a tool for **emotional healing, psychic restoration, and courageous introspection**—a way to embrace their full spectrum without self-destruction.

◈ Hemp for Emotional Healing and Shadow Work

Scorpio's emotional body is complex and layered. They often carry deep wounds from betrayal, abandonment, or suppressed rage—yet outwardly appear composed or guarded. Hemp supports Scorpio's emotional processes by **soothing the nervous system**, enhancing inner awareness, and facilitating catharsis without overwhelm.

◈ Recommended Strain Profiles for Scorpio

1. **Indica-Dominant CBD Strains**
   - Ground emotional storms with a sedative, calming effect
   - Create a safe, cocoon-like space for trauma processing and grief work
2. **Full-Spectrum CBD Extracts with THC-A (non-psychoactive)**
   - Provide full-body relief and somatic presence without intoxication
   - Ideal for meditative or therapeutic rituals
3. **Terpenes for Scorpio**
   - **Myrcene**: Deeply relaxing, supports emotional release
   - **Linalool**: Reduces tension and enhances introspective depth
   - **Nerolidol**: Known for its sedative properties and connection to lucid dreaming

◈ Ideal Product Types for Emotional Healing

- **CBD tinctures** taken before journaling or therapy sessions
- **Topical hemp oils** for chest and pelvic massage during breath-work
- **Slow-release hemp capsules** for regulating mood during long emotional cycles
- **Hemp + adaptogen elixirs** (with reishi, ashwagandha, or passionflower) to restore emotional stability

⬦ Meditative Rituals and Inner Work for Scorpio

Scorpio's domain is the **underworld of the psyche**—the hidden layers of truth, power, and purpose that most fear to face. Hemp allows Scorpio to enter these spaces with **clarity, courage, and containment**, making it easier to sit with discomfort and emerge transformed.

⬦ Ritual 1: The Scorpion's Descent – Guided Shadow Meditation

Preparation:

- Diffuse **CBD oil with vetiver or frankincense**
- Ingest a small dose of a **hemp tincture blended with blue lotus or skullcap**
- Sit in a darkened room with only candlelight or salt lamps

Process:

- Close the eyes and breathe deeply into the pelvic bowl
- Envision descending into a sacred cave inside your body
- Use prompts like:

What truth am I not speaking? What wound am I afraid to heal? What power am I hiding from?

Integration:

- Journal your discoveries, no matter how raw
- Take a warm **CBD + Epsom salt bath** with black tourmaline or obsidian stones
- End with the affirmation:

"I am whole in my light and my shadow."

◈ **Ritual 2: Scorpio's Sacred Rebirth – Moon Cycle Healing**

Scorpio's transformation often aligns with **lunar cycles**—particularly the **new moon** (release) and **full moon** (revelation). Hemp supports energetic detoxification and the embodiment of new personal truths.

New Moon Practice:

- Write down emotional patterns to release
- Burn them in a **hemp paper scroll** as a symbolic shedding
- Ingest a **CBD + dandelion root tea** to support emotional liver detox

Full Moon Practice:

- Charge a **hemp tincture** under the moonlight
- Drink with intention, speaking affirmations of rebirth:

"I reclaim my power. I transmute pain into wisdom."

- Bathe in water infused with **roses, mugwort, and CBD drops** for divine restoration

◈ **Hemp as a Tool for Boundaries and Energetic Protection**

Scorpio's empathy can become a liability if not protected. They often **absorb the pain of others**, especially in intimate relationships. Hemp helps reinforce **emotional sovereignty**, acting as a buffer against toxic entanglement.

Tools for Energetic Protection

- **CBD roll-ons at throat and solar plexus chakras** before emotionally charged interactions
- **Daily use of hemp-based aura sprays** with clary sage and rosemary
- **Hemp seed oil massage after work or public events** to clear residual energies
- Carry **hemp salves infused with black pepper or cinnamon** for boundary reinforcement when physical touch is draining

◈ **Relationship Healing and Intimacy Repair**

Scorpio rules **sexuality, intimacy, and psychological trust**. When betrayed or hurt, they retreat into silence or vengeance. Hemp offers a way to **soften the armor, access vulnerability, and repair intimacy wounds**—either solo or with a partner.

Suggested Intimacy Ritual with Hemp

- Begin with a **heart-opening CBD cacao drink**
- Light **hemp-based incense or candles** with rose or sandalwood
- Share a 10-minute **silent gaze or mirrored breathwork session**
- Apply **CBD-infused massage oil** to each other's hands, back, or feet
- End with reflective journaling on what truth emerged and what forgiveness (if any) is ready

This practice isn't about quick healing—it's about **deepening honesty and mutual reclamation** of power and pleasure.

◈ **Conclusion: Hemp as the Phoenix's Flame**

Scorpio does not fear the dark. It **becomes light through the dark**. It dies and is reborn. It hurts and becomes stronger. Hemp mirrors this alchemical journey—offering tools to navigate grief, explore truth, and emerge whole.

Whether used in solitude, ritual, therapy, or sacred relationship, hemp helps Scorpio transform pain into power. Not by numbing emotion, but by holding it gently, burning it slowly, and composting it into wisdom.

Chapter 11: Sagittarius – The Philosophical Explorer

Elevating Adventure, Expanding Thought, and Embracing Freedom with Hemp

◈ The Essence of Sagittarius

Sagittarius, the ninth sign of the zodiac, is the **cosmic traveler, visionary philosopher, and eternal seeker of truth**. Ruled by **Jupiter**, the planet of expansion, optimism, and higher wisdom, Sagittarius governs the realms of **travel, philosophy, religion, higher education, and big-picture thinking**. Those born between November 22 and December 21 are spirited wanderers, restless scholars, and storytellers of the wide unknown.

With a natural desire to **break boundaries and question convention**, Sagittarians are driven by exploration—of both the physical world and the realms of thought. They're at home on distant mountaintops, in crowded libraries, or around fireside debates. However, their love of freedom can also lead to **burnout, distraction, overcommitment, or escapism**.

Hemp, especially sativa-dominant or adaptogen-enhanced forms, is an ideal ally for Sagittarius. It supports **alertness during travel, philosophical inspiration, and calming during overstimulation**. Through intentional hemp use, Sagittarius can balance their fiery drive for expansion with clarity, presence, and self-care.

◈ Sativa-Dominant Strains for Adventurous Thought

Sagittarius requires mental stimulation like air. They thrive in movement, conversation, debate, and discovery—but without grounding, they can scatter their energy or exhaust their vitality. Sativa-dominant hemp strains offer **elevated cognition, mood enhancement, and mental flexibility**—a perfect match for the philosopher-explorer.

◈ Recommended Hemp Strain Profiles for Sagittarius

1. **Sativa-Dominant CBD Strains**
   - Promote energy, creativity, and cognitive stamina
   - Enhance philosophical focus and free-association thinking
   - Prevent mental fatigue during long lectures or travels
2. **1:1 CBD-THC Sativa Hybrids (Legal Regions)**
   - Support expansive thought without racing anxiety
   - Best for Sagittarians writing, teaching, or leading visionary projects
3. **Terpenes for Sagittarius**
   - **Pinene**: Enhances memory and mental clarity—perfect for learning and storytelling
   - **Limonene**: Elevates mood and encourages optimism
   - **Terpinolene**: Promotes creative thinking and sensory exploration

◇ **Ideal Product Types**

- **Hemp vape pens with bright citrus or pine flavor**—for quick inspiration before writing or hiking
- **CBD brain-boosting tinctures** with nootropics like bacopa or ginkgo
- **CBD energy bars** or trail snacks for sustained mental and physical performance
- **Infused adaptogen capsules** for long-distance travelers or nomads (ashwagandha + CBD + rhodiola)

◈ Hemp While Traveling: Grounding the Wanderer

Sagittarius is ruled by motion. They are the zodiac's **global citizen**, often happiest while crossing borders, meeting new cultures, and absorbing wisdom through experience. Travel, however, can also introduce jet lag, digestive disruption, anxiety, and energetic fatigue. Hemp provides vital **balance, recovery, and nervous system regulation** on the road.

◈ Travel-Friendly Hemp Rituals for Sagittarius

1. **CBD Sublingual Strips or Tablets**
   - Easy to pack, discreet, and fast-acting
   - Ideal for airport stress, long layovers, or crowded environments
2. **Portable CBD Face Mist or Essential Oil Roller**
   - Apply to temples, wrists, or neck before boarding or after a long drive
   - Uplifts mood and refreshes travel-worn skin
3. **CBD-Infused Sleep Gummies or Teas**
   - Reset circadian rhythm in new time zones
   - Encourage deep sleep while maintaining mental sharpness the next day
4. **CBD Topical Relief Balm**
   - Soothe muscle aches or back tension from long flights or hikes
   - Blend with arnica, turmeric, or peppermint for extra circulation benefits

Sagittarius Travel Mantra:
"Every destination expands me. My body remains my home."

◈ Hemp and the Pursuit of Truth

Sagittarius is the archetype of the **sage, theologian, and cultural philosopher**. Their fire burns brightest when engaging in spirited discourse, mind-expanding books, or spiritual journeys. Hemp helps Sagittarius **focus without rigidity, expand without fragmentation**, and tune into insights that integrate heart, mind, and cosmos.

Suggested Philosophical Practices with Hemp

1. Reading & Journaling Ritual

- Brew **CBD tea infused with cinnamon or cardamom**
- Light a **hemp-scented candle or incense**
- Journal using prompts like:

"What belief limits my freedom?"
"What truth have I outgrown?"
"What idea sets my spirit on fire?"

2. Outdoor Walking Meditations

- Use a **CBD tincture drop under the tongue** before a sunrise or sunset walk
- Walk slowly and consciously, asking questions aloud or silently
- Let insights arrive like arrows mid-flight—intuitive, rapid, and piercing

3. Debates or Group Dialogue

- Offer **CBD-infused drinks or chocolates** to a group of seekers or students
- Use **hemp as a social bridge**, allowing open-mindedness and laughter
- Embrace Socratic questioning while anchoring to breath and body

◈ Emotional Regulation and Freedom Maintenance

Although outwardly jovial and extroverted, Sagittarius can struggle with **emotional avoidance, overconfidence, or erratic emotional surges**—especially when they feel trapped, judged, or misunderstood. Hemp aids in processing emotions **without restricting their freedom-loving nature.**

Tools for Emotional Grounding

- **CBD bath bombs or shower melts** with sage, ginger, or cedarwood to release mental stress
- **CBD body lotion after travel** to reconnect with physical sensation
- **Evening CBD capsule + magnesium** blend to soothe racing thoughts or self-judgment
- **Affirmation ritual** after applying hemp oil to the feet:

"I trust the path. I carry wisdom and joy wherever I go."

◇ Sagittarius and the Global Green Movement

Sagittarius also cares deeply about **collective truth and global justice**. They are often drawn to hemp not only for personal use but as a **symbol of sustainable progress, liberation, and cross-cultural healing**.

Encourage Sagittarians to:

- **Support global hemp agriculture** through ethical brands
- Use **hemp-based products while abroad** to reduce plastic and chemical consumption
- Advocate for hemp education and legalization as part of their philosophical mission
- Integrate hemp in their vision of a **just, regenerative future**

◇ Conclusion: Hemp as Compass and Companion

Sagittarius is the blazing arrow—aimed at truth, fired from the heart. But even the boldest seeker needs rest, reflection, and ritual. Hemp supports this journey not by grounding the fire, but by giving it **direction, rhythm, and renewal**.

Through thoughtful strain selection, travel rituals, and expansive meditative practices, hemp becomes the Sagittarius explorer's most loyal travel companion. It supports wild wisdom with presence, fuels spiritual inquiry, and reminds the Archer that **freedom begins within**.

Chapter 12: Capricorn – The Disciplined Achiever

Building Endurance, Easing Pressure, and Balancing Ambition with Hemp

◈ The Essence of Capricorn

Capricorn, the tenth sign of the zodiac, represents the **mountain climber, architect, and master of long-term strategy**. Ruled by **Saturn**, the planet of time, responsibility, and structure, Capricorn governs ambition, endurance, legacy, and discipline. Those born between December 22 and January 19 often appear composed, pragmatic, and success-oriented—deeply committed to their goals and purpose.

Capricorns are builders: of businesses, empires, institutions, and identities. They value **integrity, self-mastery, and tangible achievement**. Yet beneath their strength lies immense inner pressure. Many Capricorns carry **heavy expectations**, push themselves beyond exhaustion, and suffer in silence—rarely asking for help.

Hemp offers Capricorn what they rarely give themselves: **permission to soften**, restore, and breathe. It supports **mental clarity, muscular tension release, and structured self-care**. With hemp as a ritual companion, Capricorn can maintain their momentum without burnout and find stillness that reinforces—not sabotages—their success.

◈ **Hemp for Focus, Productivity, and Tension Relief**

Capricorn's greatest assets—discipline, responsibility, ambition—can become burdens when unbalanced. Hemp helps maintain a **state of high functionality** while preventing collapse from stress or overexertion. The right formulations can enhance **mental sharpness, muscle recovery, and calm under pressure.**

◈ **Recommended Strain Profiles for Capricorn**

1. **High-CBD Sativa-Hybrids**
   - Promote sustained focus during work or planning
   - Reduce tension headaches and mental fatigue
   - Maintain clarity without sedation
2. **Balanced 1:1 CBD-THC (or CBD + CBG) Formulations**
   - Ideal for physical recovery after work or workouts
   - Support both cognition and bodily ease for high-performance individuals
3. **Terpenes for Capricorn**
   - **Beta-Caryophyllene**: Anti-inflammatory, tension-relieving, and grounding
   - **Humulene**: Appetite suppressant and energy stabilizer
   - **Pinene**: Promotes memory, focus, and clear planning

◈ **Productivity-Enhancing Hemp Products**

- **CBD tinctures with lion's mane or ginseng** for focused execution
- **Infused roll-ons** for shoulder and neck tightness from desk work
- **Hemp-based compression creams** for joint stiffness or chronic pain
- **CBD adaptogen capsules** (ashwagandha, rhodiola, reishi) for stress endurance

◈ Structured Relaxation for the Responsible Soul

Capricorn often struggles with the concept of rest—seeing it as laziness or loss of time. Hemp invites **intentional restoration**, integrating downtime into their schedule as a **strategic investment** in longevity and excellence.

◈ Scheduled Self-Care Rituals with Hemp

Morning Ritual: Grounded Clarity

- Apply **CBD-infused face cream or eye serum** while setting your intentions
- Ingest a **low-dose hemp tincture** with matcha or black tea to activate alertness

Midday Reset: Mental Realignment

- Use a **CBD aromatherapy pen** with peppermint or rosemary
- Stretch or take a short walk while microdosing a **CBD gummy or lozenge**

Evening Ritual: Body Repair and Inner Decompression

- Take a **warm magnesium + hemp oil bath soak** with forest essential oils
- Rub **CBD muscle salve** into knees, shoulders, or lower back
- End with a calming tea blend (chamomile, valerian, hemp flower) while journaling

Capricorn thrives on efficiency—so this structure reassures them that **rest can also serve achievement**.

◈♂ Hemp for Stamina and Physical Recovery

Capricorns tend to push through physical discomfort to meet deadlines or goals. Over time, this can manifest as **chronic back tension, joint inflammation, adrenal fatigue**, or muscular rigidity. Hemp provides an **intelligent support system for performance, longevity, and recovery**.

Physical Restoration Practices with Hemp

- **CBD Protein Shakes or Recovery Bars** post-workout or workday
- **Topical hemp creams with menthol or camphor** for stiff joints or stress knots
- **CBD foot soaks** after long hours of standing or walking
- **Full-spectrum CBD oil + turmeric capsules** to reduce inflammation systemically

Capricorn's body responds well to routines that are both **regimented and nourishing**. Hemp becomes a vital component in a Capricorn's maintenance plan—like brushing teeth, saving money, or showing up to work.

◈ Mental Fortitude and Emotional Balance

While Capricorn appears emotionally stoic, they often battle **internalized stress, pessimism, or guilt**. Saturn's influence can lead to **feelings of failure, inadequacy, or emotional suppression**, especially when they don't meet their own high standards. Hemp invites **emotional honesty, gentle self-compassion, and nonjudgmental presence**.

Emotional Integration Ritual

Step 1: Quiet Reflection

- Inhale **CBD-rich essential oil blend** of spruce, vetiver, and lavender
- Sit in a dark room with calming music or silence

Step 2: Breath-Body Awareness

- Inhale for 4 counts, hold for 7, exhale for 8
- Visualize pressure leaving the body with each breath

Step 3: Journal Prompt + Hemp Support

- Take a small **CBD + ashwagandha tincture**
- Journal using prompts like:

"Where am I holding pressure that doesn't belong to me?"
"What do I need to feel safe and supported?"
This practice gives Capricorn permission to slow down, release judgment, and reclaim **inner authority without harshness**.

◈ Hemp as a Strategic Investment

Capricorns are naturally drawn to **long-term thinking**—including in health, productivity, and ethical responsibility. They appreciate data, results, and consistency. Hemp fits seamlessly into their ethos when framed not as indulgence, but as a **functional, sustainable wellness investment.**

Capricorn's Smart Uses of Hemp

- Track effects in a **habit journal or planner** (mood, focus, sleep, recovery)
- Create a **CBD budget line item** for high-quality, science-backed products
- Incorporate hemp into goal-setting retreats or quarterly reviews
- Gift hemp products to team members, clients, or family as stress-relief tools

◈ Conclusion: Hemp as Capricorn's Quiet Ally

Capricorn doesn't need shortcuts. They need **sustainable fuel, strategic recovery, and clear structure**. Hemp becomes a quiet but loyal ally—reinforcing Capricorn's discipline with compassion, easing tension without sacrificing sharpness, and helping them climb without crumbling.

Chapter 13: Aquarius – The Visionary Reformer

Innovating Wellness, Rewiring Rituals, and Advancing Humanity Through Hemp

◈ The Essence of Aquarius

Aquarius, the eleventh sign of the zodiac, is the **cosmic futurist, radical thinker, and humanitarian of the stars**. Ruled by **Uranus**, the planet of innovation, disruption, and awakening, and co-ruled in traditional astrology by **Saturn**, Aquarius governs **technology, collective movements, originality, and systems change**. Those born between January 20 and February 18 often carry a natural genius, a rebellious streak, and a devotion to improving the world through intellect, equality, and experimentation.

Aquarius is the **sign of progressive evolution**—the mind that moves ahead of its time and the heart that beats for the greater good. However, their brilliant detachment can also lead to **emotional distance, nervous tension, and inconsistent self-care**. Hemp offers Aquarius a grounding framework to **embody their vision**, regulate mental energy, and contribute to social wellness in meaningful, unconventional ways.

◈ Innovative Hemp Tech and Social Change Products

Aquarius thrives at the intersection of **science, ethics, and innovation**. They are drawn to cutting-edge applications of nature—especially when these advances serve a **collective purpose**. Hemp, with its regenerative properties and endless uses, mirrors Aquarius's idealism and ingenuity.

◈ Futuristic Hemp Applications That Speak to Aquarius

1. **Bioplastic and Hemp-Based Textiles**
   - Used in ethical fashion, packaging, and even architectural materials
   - Reflect Aquarius's commitment to sustainability and circular design
2. **Nano-Emulsified CBD**
   - Advanced absorption technology that maximizes bioavailability
   - Perfect for Aquarians interested in quantified wellness and precision dosing
3. **Wearable Hemp Devices**
   - Smart CBD patches or biofeedback tools with hemp infusion
   - Bridge tech with plant medicine for integrated daily performance
4. **Community Hemp Farming Co-ops**
   - Aquarians may be drawn to **democratizing access** through urban gardens, collective cultivation, or open-source education projects

◈ **Suggested Products for the Aquarian Archetype**

* **Lab-verified CBD nootropic blends** for productivity and vision mapping
* **Zero-waste hemp skincare** in refillable packaging
* **Hemp meditation mats or yoga props** made from recycled fiber
* **Infused beverages designed for social events and brain-storming meetups**

Aquarius sees hemp not as a trend, but as a **revolutionary tool**—a catalyst for eco-conscious culture shifts and future-ready well-being.

◈ **Personalized Blends for Unique Minds**

Aquarians are **highly individualistic**, often resistant to one-size-fits-all health advice. They seek **customization, freedom, and intellectual stimulation**, even in their rituals. Hemp's versatility allows Aquarius to craft **tailored blends** that align with their ever-evolving mental states and creative experiments.

◈ **DIY Hemp Ritual Kits for Aquarius**

1. **CBD + Brain Booster Elixir**
   - Blend CBD isolate with schisandra, lion's mane, and blue lotus
   - Use before creative writing, innovation sprints, or research deep dives
2. **Evening Wind-Down Blend**
   - Full-spectrum CBD, lemon balm, and passionflower tincture
   - Designed to balance Aquarius's overactive mind before bed
3. **Vapor Ritual for Mental Clarity**
   - Sativa-dominant hemp vape with essential oils: eucalyptus, rosemary, and peppermint
   - Best used during collaborative meetings or planning sessions
4. **Community Care Tea Formula**
   - CBD hemp flower, hibiscus, nettle, and elderflower
   - Brewed in groups, shared in circles to build intentional community presence

◈ Hemp in Community Rituals and Visionary Circles

Despite their iconoclastic nature, Aquarius is deeply driven by **collective healing**. They long for **communities based on equality, truth, and mutual evolution**. Hemp becomes a symbol of **planetary citizenship and non-hierarchical wisdom**—a plant that nourishes the many, not the few.

◈ Community-Based Rituals for the Aquarian Soul

1. Vision Council Gatherings

- Gather changemakers, activists, and thinkers
- Begin with a **CBD tea ceremony**
- Discuss community solutions while passing a shared herbal vapor blend
- Close with co-created affirmations or a collective vision board

2. Urban Hemp Garden Blessings

- Celebrate planting or harvest cycles
- Each participant offers an intention as they sow hemp seeds
- Incorporate **CBD-infused salves or sprays** as part of blessing rituals

3. Solstice or Equinox Healing Pods

- Host seasonal events with music, movement, and intentional hemp integration
- Include **CBD-infused art stations, tarot + hemp pairings**, or **zodiac-aligned herbal baths**

4. Digital Rituals

- Aquarians may also host **virtual hemp meditations** using digital sound baths and mailed ritual kits
- Integrate **AR (augmented reality)** or livestream experiences with hemp wellness education

Aquarius is the sign most likely to **reimagine spirituality and health as decentralized, co-created, and future-proof.**

◈ Nervous System Balance for the Overclocked Mind

Aquarians often live **in their heads**—innovating, thinking, and solving abstract problems 24/7. This cerebral electricity can manifest as **insomnia, anxiety, dissociation, or emotional fragmentation.** Hemp becomes the anchor that gently pulls Aquarius **back into the body**—not to confine them, but to **support their genius sustainably.**

Tools to Reconnect Body and Mind

- **CBD body oil applied to the calves and ankles** (Aquarius-ruled areas)
- **Guided breathwork with microdosed hemp elixir** before brainstorming sessions
- **Digital detox + hemp ritual baths** to restore parasympathetic balance
- **CBD + B-complex supplement stacks** to replenish nervous system support

Aquarian Grounding Mantra
"My mind is a beacon, my body the power station. Together, they illuminate change."

◈ Conclusion: Hemp as the Future's Frequency

Aquarius is here to **update the world**, and hemp is part of that operating system. Together, they represent an era where **plant wisdom meets technological insight**, where healing becomes democratic, and where rituals are as decentralized and inventive as the people who perform them.

Through personalized blends, community innovations, and progressive science-backed uses, hemp helps Aquarius stay **creative, balanced, and aligned with their mission to reform, revolutionize, and reimagine a better world.**

Chapter 14: Pisces – The Mystic Dreamer

Embracing Empathy, Enhancing Intuition, and Elevating Dreams with Hemp

◈ The Essence of Pisces

Pisces, the twelfth and final sign of the zodiac, represents **completion, transcendence, compassion, and the mystical unknown.** Ruled by **Neptune**, the planet of dreams, illusion, intuition, and the spiritual realm, Pisces governs **imagination, healing, psychic sensitivity, and the dissolving of egoic boundaries**. Those born between February 19 and March 20 often appear dreamy, deeply empathetic, artistic, and attuned to invisible energies that others overlook.

Pisces is the **ether of the zodiac**—fluid, emotional, and spiritually porous. While this sensitivity allows for divine creativity and soul-level compassion, it can also open the door to **overwhelm, escapism, and emotional exhaustion**. Hemp offers a sacred bridge: helping Pisces **stay grounded while enhancing their intuitive gifts**, calming their overactive energy without dimming their inner light.

When used mindfully, hemp becomes the gentle anchor Pisces needs to thrive in both the seen and unseen worlds—supporting emotional clarity, dream work, and inspired expression.

◈ Soothing Hemp for Intuition and Artistry

Pisces is naturally tuned to **subtle emotional frequencies and imaginative flow**. Yet this attunement can blur personal boundaries, making it difficult for Pisces to know where they end and others begin. Hemp supports Pisces in **creating energetic definition** while nurturing their visionary instincts.

◈ Ideal Strain Profiles for Pisces

1. **CBD-Rich Indicas with Mild Sedative Effects**
   - Promote calm without suppressing psychic or creative flow
   - Assist with emotional clarity and energetic protection
2. **Balanced 1:1 CBD-THC Blends (in legal areas)**
   - Deepen artistic focus and sensory engagement
   - Facilitate immersion into poetry, music, or trance states
3. **Terpenes for Pisces**
   - **Linalool**: Encourages emotional tranquility and dream enhancement
   - **Myrcene**: Soothes nervous tension and improves sleep
   - **Nerolidol**: Supports vivid dreaming and deeper meditative states

◈ Hemp Pairings for Creative Practices

- **Hemp-infused watercolor or calligraphy sessions** for emotional release
- **CBD teas with jasmine or rose** while composing music, poetry, or dream journals
- **Topical hemp oil on temples and wrists** before engaging in intuitive readings, tarot, or visualization work
- **CBD lozenges** for grounding during emotionally intense performances or public displays of art

Pisces thrives when their environment supports **gentle sensory input and emotional flow**—and hemp becomes a trusted creative muse and psychic balm.

◈ Aromatherapy and Dream Enhancement

As the zodiac's dreamwalker, Pisces naturally dwells in the liminal spaces between waking and sleeping, memory and vision, fantasy and intuition. Hemp supports the **transition into these altered states** with grace, helping Pisces access their unconscious mind without losing their grounding.

◈ Hemp Rituals for Enhanced Dreaming

1. Lucid Dream Support Ritual
Preparation:

- Brew a **CBD + mugwort tea** 30–45 minutes before bed
- Place a **drop of full-spectrum CBD oil on the third eye**
- Use a hemp-infused essential oil blend in a diffuser with sandalwood, lavender, and clary sage

Bedside Affirmation:
"I welcome sacred dreams and trust in their truth."

Integration:

- Keep a dream journal at your bedside
- Upon waking, record dream symbols, emotions, and guidance
- Reflect weekly to notice patterns or messages

2. Intuitive Visualization Practice

Pisces can tap into visions and non-verbal truths with remarkable ease. Hemp heightens **sensitivity to symbolic language and archetypal imagery**, allowing deeper access to messages from the subconscious or spiritual planes.

Steps:

- Begin with a **small dose of CBD tincture or vapor inhalation**
- Close your eyes and breathe deeply, focusing on your heart space
- Envision a sacred ocean, allowing images, beings, or messages to rise organically
- Ask:

"What is my soul trying to express?"
"Where does my spirit need nourishment?"

Post-Session:

- Use colored pencils or paints to capture what you saw or felt
- Apply **hemp hand cream or balm** to seal the experience into your senses

◈ Emotional Regulation and Energetic Boundaries

Pisces feels everything. Their porous emotional nature means they can absorb others' emotions, dreams, or traumas without realizing it. Hemp helps **establish energetic filters**, so Pisces can offer compassion without depletion.

Daily Energetic Hygiene with Hemp

- **CBD bath salts with seaweed or lavender** after emotionally intense days
- Apply **topical hemp oil to soles of the feet** to bring awareness back to the body
- Diffuse **CBD-infused aromatherapy mist** while performing cord-cutting rituals
- Wear **hemp-seed oil blended with sage or palo santo** to strengthen boundaries in public or spiritual spaces

Piscean Grounding Mantra:
"I can feel deeply and remain whole. I receive only what serves me."

◈ Compassionate Living and Collective Healing

Pisces is the sign of **universal love and spiritual unity**. They're drawn to causes that alleviate suffering, heal communities, and express the soul's longing for peace. Hemp reflects Pisces's commitment to **healing the planet and dissolving division**—not as an escape, but as a restoration of harmony.

Hemp as a Spiritual and Humanitarian Tool

- Volunteer in **hemp-based wellness programs** for trauma survivors or mental health outreach
- Host **Pisces-themed full moon gatherings** using hemp as a sacred offering
- Lead **collective meditations or sound baths** paired with calming hemp teas
- Donate to **eco-conscious hemp initiatives** supporting indigenous farming, clean water, or social equity

Pisces knows that true healing is not just personal—it's planetary. Hemp becomes both **vessel and voice** for their compassion.

◈ Conclusion: Hemp as Portal to Inner Oceans

Pisces is the final note in the zodiac's cosmic symphony—the mystic who dissolves into stars, songs, and sacred waters. But even dreamers need **ritual, grounding, and containment**. Hemp provides the softness Pisces craves and the strength they forget they possess.

Through dreamwork, aromatherapy, creative rituals, and daily emotional cleansing, hemp becomes Pisces's **trusted guide across inner oceans**—a reminder that spirituality and sensitivity are not weaknesses, but gifts meant to be honored and held with care.

Chapter 15: Moon Phases and Hemp

Harnessing Lunar Rhythms for Cultivation, Healing, and Ritual Transformation

⟡ The Moon as a Celestial Timekeeper

Since ancient times, the Moon has been revered as the **primordial clock of nature**—marking rhythms of growth, rest, transformation, and renewal. Across civilizations, lunar phases have guided **planting seasons, spiritual rituals, emotional reflection**, and feminine cycles. The Moon's gravitational pull doesn't just affect the tides—it subtly shifts **the waters within us**, influencing intuition, sleep, emotions, and the energy of the plants we grow and consume.

Hemp, a plant deeply rooted in the earth yet highly responsive to environmental cues, thrives under lunar guidance. Whether you're cultivating hemp, crafting rituals, or consuming hemp-based products, aligning your practices with the **Moon's eight phases** can amplify potency, intention, and spiritual resonance.

This chapter explores how to work harmoniously with the Moon—both agriculturally and personally—bringing together **astrological wisdom, herbal magick, and hemp ritual** for balanced living.

◈ Hemp Cultivation by Lunar Phase

Lunar agriculture, sometimes called **biodynamic planting**, follows the principle that **sap flow, germination, and root development** are all influenced by the Moon's gravitational shifts. By syncing hemp cultivation practices with the Moon, growers can optimize **yield, resin quality, cannabinoid potency**, and plant vitality.

◈ 1. New Moon – Germination and Intention

- **Moon energy:** Internalized, fertile, mysterious
- **Hemp cultivation:** Sow hemp seeds just after the New Moon to harness building lunar energy. Root growth is strong during this dark, yin phase.
- **Ritual tip:** Write an intention on hemp parchment and bury it with the seeds

◈ 2. Waxing Crescent – Root Strength and Structure

- **Moon energy:** Building momentum, planning, grounding
- **Hemp cultivation:** Ideal for applying **root enhancers or microbial fertilizers**. The plant focuses below the surface.
- **Ritual tip:** Tend to intentions daily with light, water, and whispered affirmations

◈ 3. First Quarter – Strength and Stability

- **Moon energy:** Action, decision, inner strength
- **Hemp cultivation:** Begin pruning or supporting stalks. Transplant seedlings during this phase for resilience.
- **Ritual tip:** Charge your cultivation tools (scissors, gloves) under moonlight

◈ 4. Waxing Gibbous – Nutrient Uptake and Vitality

- **Moon energy:** Refined growth, readiness, heightened sensitivity
- **Hemp cultivation:** Apply top-layer fertilizers or compost teas. The plant pulls nutrients upward during this juicy phase.
- **Ritual tip:** Bless your plants with infused moon water (hemp leaf + quartz in spring water)

◈ 5. Full Moon – Flowering, Potency, and Harvest

- **Moon energy:** Illumination, culmination, maximum energy
- **Hemp cultivation:** Flowering is optimal under full light. Begin light-sensitive techniques like adjusting light cycles for indoor grows.
- **Ritual tip:** Harvest for **maximum CBD and terpene potency** within 1–3 days of the Full Moon. Conduct gratitude ceremonies with your plants.

◈ 6. Waning Gibbous – Integration and Preservation

- **Moon energy:** Gratitude, learning, sharing
- **Hemp cultivation:** Begin slow-drying harvested flowers. This phase supports nutrient redistribution and terpene maturation.
- **Ritual tip:** Create herbal bundles or dry leaves for future teas and incense

◈ 7. Last Quarter – Composting and Clearing

- **Moon energy:** Release, purification, surrender
- **Hemp cultivation:** Remove failed stalks, compost, and clear debris from your grow space. Prepare the soil for future cycles.
- **Ritual tip:** Burn hemp incense to cleanse growing areas or ritual altars

◈ 8. Waning Crescent – Rest and Restoration

- **Moon energy:** Silence, dreaming, preparation for rebirth
- **Hemp cultivation:** Allow the land to rest. Avoid planting. Reflect on what worked and what didn't.
- **Ritual tip:** Perform dreamwork rituals using **CBD teas or tinctures** blended with chamomile or mugwort

◈ Personal Hemp Rituals Aligned with the Moon

The Moon's emotional and energetic influence can also be mirrored in **personal wellness rituals** involving hemp. By aligning self-care, creativity, and spiritual practices with each phase, you create a **living ritual calendar** that brings balance to mind, body, and spirit.

◈ New Moon – Initiate and Reflect

- **Focus:** Set new intentions; plant inner seeds
- **Hemp ritual:** Take a microdose of **CBD isolate** and sit in quiet meditation. Write goals or dreams on hemp paper.
- **Aromatherapy:** Hemp-infused balm with clove, patchouli, or sandalwood

◈ First Quarter – Act and Adjust

- **Focus:** Make decisions, initiate movement
- **Hemp ritual:** Use a **CBD roll-on** before a workout or creative endeavor. Practice breathwork to build momentum.
- **Bath ritual:** Epsom salt + hemp soak to strengthen body/mind resolve

◈ Full Moon – Celebrate and Release

- **Focus:** Shine light on truth, complete cycles
- **Hemp ritual:** Perform a **CBD cacao ceremony** under moonlight. Share dreams with a trusted circle. Dance or journal freely.
- **Smoke ritual:** Hemp flower in a ceremonial pipe to commune with spirit

◈ Last Quarter – Let Go and Cleanse

- **Focus:** Release habits, relationships, or thought patterns
- **Hemp ritual:** Use **CBD tincture with lemon balm** to ease emotional release. Perform cord-cutting rituals with hemp rope or thread.
- **Space clearing:** Burn dried hemp leaves with rosemary and cedar

◈ Moon + Zodiac Combinations for Hemp Rituals

Every New and Full Moon occurs in a zodiac sign—adding an **astrological flavor** to your rituals. Enhance your lunar work with **zodiac-matched hemp pairings**:

Moon Sign	Ritual Energy	Ideal Hemp Use
Aries	Action, courage	Sativa-dominant CBD for motivation
Taurus	Pleasure, embodiment	Hemp-infused massage and edible indulgence
Gemini	Communication, duality	CBD teas with stimulating adaptogens
Cancer	Nurturing, emotional release	Warm CBD baths and comfort-focused rituals
Leo	Expression, pride	CBD + creativity sessions or stage performance
Virgo	Cleansing, structure	Topical CBD routines and gut-supporting blends
Libra	Balance, beauty	CBD facials and relationship ceremonies

Moon Sign	Ritual Energy	Ideal Hemp Use
Scorpio	Depth, shadow work	Dream journaling with hemp and blue lotus
Sagittarius	Wisdom, expansion	CBD before travel or philosophical meditation
Capricorn	Discipline, legacy	CBD productivity planners and body relief
Aquarius	Innovation, collective change	Group CBD rituals and tech-infused practices
Pisces	Intuition, dreams	Aromatherapy, sleep teas, and spiritual art

◈ Conclusion: Moonlight as Medicine, Hemp as Ritual

Just as hemp responds to the tides of the moon, so do we. In syncing our **intentions, actions, and wellness practices** to lunar rhythms, we rediscover an ancient truth: **the body is cosmic, and nature speaks in cycles**.

Let hemp be your sacred herb for emotional tides, your lunar companion in healing, and your grounding tool during spiritual peaks and valleys. Whether planting seeds in soil or in the soul, let the Moon guide you, and let hemp support your becoming.

Chapter 16: Planetary Alignment and Hemp Healing

Synchronizing Celestial Forces with Earth-Based Remedies for Holistic Wellness

◈ The Cosmic Influence on Plants and People

Since ancient times, astrologers, herbalists, and alchemists have understood that the **planets are not distant or disconnected** from life on Earth. Instead, they are **living energies**—celestial archetypes that influence our emotional states, bodily functions, and the vibrational fields of plants. In this holistic view, healing is most effective when timed with the planetary currents, integrating the movement of the cosmos with the tools of the earth.

Hemp, as a highly adaptive and spiritually intelligent plant, is especially receptive to planetary energies. Its cannabinoids, terpenes, and healing properties can be **activated, enhanced, or harmonized** through proper astrological timing and ritual design. When we work with hemp during specific planetary alignments, we aren't just treating symptoms—we are **engaging a multidimensional healing process** that honors both the cosmic and the corporeal.

◈ How Planetary Energy Affects Hemp and Healing

Each planet in our solar system emits a **unique energetic frequency** that corresponds to particular bodily systems, emotional archetypes, and herbal allies. These energies subtly influence the effectiveness of healing tools, including hemp. Understanding planetary rulership helps determine when and how to prepare, consume, or anoint with hemp for **maximum spiritual, mental, and physical benefit.**

◈ Sun – Vitality and Self-Identity

- **Influence on hemp:** Boosts confidence, supports solar plexus work, enhances CBD's energizing potential
- **Hemp timing:** Use during midday rituals or when the Sun is in Leo or Aries
- **Remedy focus:** Uplifting salves, golden-hued hemp oils, and solar-charged CBD teas

◈ Moon – Emotions and Intuition

- **Influence on hemp:** Deepens emotional healing, calms the nervous system, enhances dreamwork
- **Hemp timing:** Full Moon, New Moon, or when Moon is in Cancer or Pisces
- **Remedy focus:** Sleep blends, CBD bath bombs, dream-enhancement oils

☿ Mercury – Communication and Clarity

- **Influence on hemp:** Improves focus, mental clarity, reduces anxiety from overstimulation
- **Hemp timing:** During Mercury retrogrades or when Mercury is in Gemini or Virgo
- **Remedy focus:** CBD-infused teas for brain fog, vapor blends for speaking rituals

♀ Venus – Beauty and Connection

- **Influence on hemp:** Enhances pleasure, relationships, skin care, and sensual rituals
- **Hemp timing:** When Venus is in Taurus or Libra, or during Friday rituals
- **Remedy focus:** Rose + CBD face serums, anointing oils for self-love and intimacy

♂ Mars – Action and Motivation

- **Influence on hemp:** Supports stamina, pain relief, physical endurance, and assertiveness
- **Hemp timing:** During Mars transits in Aries, Scorpio, or Capricorn
- **Remedy focus:** Muscle salves, pre-workout CBD tinctures, energizing topicals

◈ Jupiter – Expansion and Wisdom

- **Influence on hemp:** Encourages optimism, digestion, spiritual growth, and abundance rituals
- **Hemp timing:** When Jupiter is in Sagittarius or Pisces; during luck-based ceremonies
- **Remedy focus:** Hemp tonics with turmeric or ginger, gratitude journaling rituals

◈ Saturn – Structure and Discipline

- **Influence on hemp:** Promotes long-term healing, boundaries, resilience, and bone health
- **Hemp timing:** During Saturn transits in Capricorn or Aquarius
- **Remedy focus:** Grounding CBD capsules, hemp infusions for chronic pain or regulation

◈ Uranus – Innovation and Awakening

- **Influence on hemp:** Catalyzes breakthroughs, resets nervous system, inspires invention
- **Hemp timing:** When Uranus transits your natal chart; during full-moon insights
- **Remedy focus:** Technologically advanced CBD blends, micro-dosed ritual tinctures

◈ Neptune – Dreams and Spiritual Sensitivity

- **Influence on hemp:** Heightens intuition, trance states, creativity, and emotional fluidity
- **Hemp timing:** During Neptune alignments in Pisces or Cancer
- **Remedy focus:** Sleep support, creative art sessions, ritual anointments for sacred space

◈ Pluto – Transformation and Shadow Work

- **Influence on hemp:** Facilitates trauma processing, rebirth, detox, and deep psychic healing
- **Hemp timing:** Pluto returns, eclipses, or Scorpio transits
- **Remedy focus:** Dark moon rituals, CBD with activated charcoal, inner alchemy tinctures

◈ Ritual Timing and Astro-Remedy Making

By timing your hemp remedies with planetary transits, you engage in **astrological herbalism**—a sacred blend of astrology, plant wisdom, and energetic intention. The goal is not just healing, but alignment with **universal rhythms**.

◈ 1. Planetary Days and Hours

Each day of the week is ruled by a planet, offering an optimal time for hemp ritual:

Day	Planet	Ideal Hemp Use
Sunday	Sun	Confidence, visibility, CBD for self-empowerment
Monday	Moon	Intuition, sleep support, emotional regulation
Tuesday	Mars	Motivation, workouts, energizing hemp blends
Wednesday	Mercury	Focus, communication, mental clarity
Thursday	Jupiter	Abundance, learning, spiritual expansion
Friday	Venus	Beauty, love, pleasure-enhancing hemp self-care

Day	Planet	Ideal Hemp Use
Saturday	Saturn	Grounding, structure, long-term healing rituals

For deeper precision, use a **planetary hour calculator** to determine the exact ruling hour of your ritual, allowing for a layered energetic infusion.

◈ 2. Creating Astro-Aligned Hemp Remedies

To enhance your own practice, consider preparing **hemp-based as-tro-remedies** aligned to specific planetary themes:

◈ Mercury Clarity Elixir

- **Ingredients:** CBD tincture + rosemary + lemon balm + peppermint
- **Purpose:** Enhance clarity during writing, studying, or negotiations
- **Timing:** Wednesday during Mercury hour

◈ Pluto Purge Potion

- **Ingredients:** Full-spectrum CBD + activated charcoal + ginger root
- **Purpose:** Assist in trauma release, emotional detox, shadow work
- **Timing:** During Pluto retrogrades or Scorpio Moon

◈ Jupiter Expansion Tea

- **Ingredients:** Hemp leaf + turmeric + fennel + honey
- **Purpose:** Uplift mood, support digestion, and spiritual optimism
- **Timing:** Thursday morning during waxing moon

◈ Astrology + Hemp for Natal Healing

Every person has a unique birth chart with **planetary placements** that can reveal health strengths, vulnerabilities, and patterns of emotional processing. When personalized, hemp healing can be tailored to your chart:

- **Saturn in the 6th House?** Use grounding CBD blends to support chronic fatigue
- **Moon in Pisces?** Support with dream-enhancing hemp and boundaries rituals
- **Sun in Leo?** Use solar-charged CBD oils for confidence and voice expression

Your body is your sky. Every remedy becomes more powerful when it **reflects the heavens from which your energy flows.**

◈ Conclusion: Celestial Chemistry in Every Drop

Planetary alignment is not just a metaphor—it is a matrix. Hemp is a cosmic conductor that **transmits and transforms planetary energies** through our cells, senses, and spirit. With every application, infusion, or ritual, we tune our healing to the **divine clockwork** of the cosmos.

By understanding the roles of the planets and learning to time your remedies accordingly, you become an astro-alchemist—one who does not fight the current, but flows with the stars.

Let the sky speak. Let the plant translate. And let your healing begin.

Chapter 17: Daily & Seasonal Hemp Rituals

Infusing Everyday Rhythms and Seasonal Gateways with the Healing Power of Hemp

◇ Ritual as Alignment

Rituals are not merely habits—they are **intentional acts that create alignment between the inner self and the outer world**. When hemp is included in these sacred moments, it becomes more than a remedy; it becomes a bridge. A bridge between time and presence, between body and spirit, between earth and sky.

Incorporating hemp into your daily rhythm and seasonal ceremonies grounds your wellness practice into **cyclical awareness**, restoring harmony where modern life often creates disconnection. Whether through morning drops of CBD oil to greet the sun, or solstice ceremonies beneath the stars, these rituals are meant to **honor the wisdom of nature's clock and your place within it**.

This chapter offers a full system of daily and seasonal rituals—rooted in ancient timing, elevated by hemp—to help you navigate your days and years with intention, peace, and holistic wellness.

◈ **Daily Hemp Rituals: Morning, Midday & Evening**

Integrating hemp into your daily flow enhances your physical, mental, and spiritual well-being while **creating anchors of awareness** throughout the day.

◈ **Morning Rituals – Grounding Intention & Awakening the Body**

Theme: Focus, clarity, breath, empowerment

Best Products: CBD tincture (sativa-leaning or broad-spectrum), hemp-infused matcha or tea, energizing topicals

Steps:

1. **Gratitude Breathwork**
   - Take 3–5 deep breaths, placing one hand over your heart and one over your abdomen
   - Inhale: "I arrive."
   - Exhale: "I align."
2. **Hemp Application**
   - Take a dose of energizing **CBD oil** under the tongue or mix into a morning smoothie
   - Use **hemp-infused facial serum or moisturizer** to awaken skin and set tone for the day
3. **Affirmation Ritual**
   - Apply **CBD roll-on to wrists or solar plexus**, stating aloud:

"I move through this day with clarity, energy, and balance."

◈ Midday Rituals – Recharge, Refocus, Recalibrate

Theme: Productivity, digestion, mood stability
Best Products: Hemp snacks, infused beverages, cooling salves

Steps:

1. **Digestive Pause**
   - Sip **CBD herbal tea** (e.g., ginger, peppermint, or tulsi-based) to support digestion and calm mid-day nerves
   - Eat a **hemp protein snack or edible** rich in omega-3s to stabilize energy

2. **Micro-Movement + Recenter**
   - Step away from your workspace and stretch or walk outdoors
   - Apply **CBD balm** to temples or shoulders to relieve mental tension

3. **Reflection Prompt**
   - Write one sentence: *What do I need less of right now? What do I want more of?*

◈ Evening Rituals – Restoration, Release, and Sacred Sleep

Theme: Rest, emotional digestion, dream integration

Best Products: Full-spectrum or indica-leaning CBD oil, bath bombs, sleep blends

Steps:

1. **CBD Bath Soak or Foot Soak**
   - Use **Epsom salts blended with CBD and lavender or chamomile essential oil**
   - Soak to release daily energetic residue and muscle tension
2. **Night Tea + Journal**
   - Brew a calming **CBD-infused tea** with valerian root or lemon balm
   - Journal or write 3 things you're grateful for
   - Apply **CBD sleep balm to the soles of the feet** and pulse points
3. **Dream Invocation**
   - Speak softly:

"I welcome peaceful sleep and meaningful dreams."
"May hemp be my ally in crossing into the sacred night."

◈ **Seasonal Hemp Rituals: Solstices, Equinoxes, and Earth Cycles**

Throughout history, solstices and equinoxes have served as **portals of transformation**—moments when the veil between personal time and cosmic time grows thin. These are powerful opportunities for ritual, especially when integrated with plant allies like hemp, which **responds sensitively to light cycles, temperature, and Earth's energetic shifts**.

◈ **Winter Solstice – December 21**
Theme: Rest, reflection, renewal
Hemp Use: Deep relaxation, healing teas, dreamwork, inner rituals
Ritual:

- Light candles in a dark room
- Drink a warming **CBD chai blend**
- Reflect on what you're releasing from the year
- Anoint your heart with hemp oil infused with pine, clove, or frankincense

◈ **Spring Equinox – March 20**
Theme: Rebirth, creativity, new intentions
Hemp Use: Uplifting tinctures, ceremonial planting, clarity tools
Ritual:

- Plant **hemp seeds or symbolic herbs** in fresh soil
- Use a **CBD spray or roll-on** with citrus or rosemary scents
- Write out a new intention and breathe it into the earth
- Meditate on your personal springtime

◈ **Summer Solstice – June 21**
Theme: Illumination, celebration, vitality
Hemp Use: Energizing oils, creative enhancement, outdoor applications
Ritual:

- Create a **CBD and hibiscus iced tea** for vitality
- Dance, sing, or paint in natural light
- Share your abundance with others—a meal, a ritual, a story
- Use a **hemp-based sunscreen or body oil** during sunbathing or walking

◈ **Autumn Equinox – September 22**
Theme: Gratitude, preparation, balance
Hemp Use: Digestive blends, calming topicals, letting go tools
Ritual:

- Enjoy a **hemp-infused meal** with friends or family
- Use **CBD and cinnamon massage oil** to honor your body
- Write a list of what you've harvested this year—internal or external
- Perform a **smoke or incense cleansing** using dried hemp leaves and sage

◈ **Aligning Hemp to the Wheel of the Year**

For those following the **Wiccan, Pagan, or nature-based** cycles, you may also integrate hemp into the 8 Sabbats (e.g., Imbolc, Beltane, Samhain). Each turn of the wheel offers opportunities to create **custom blends, sacred body anointments, or ceremonial consumption practices** using hemp tailored to the sabbat's intention.

Example:

- **Beltane (May 1):** Use a **rose + hemp oil massage ritual** to honor love and fertility
- **Samhain (Oct 31):** Burn **hemp incense with myrrh** for ancestral connection and spirit communication

◈ **Conclusion: Living in Hemp Time**

Daily rituals are how we *remember* who we are. Seasonal rituals are how we *become* who we're meant to be. When paired with the nurturing, balancing properties of hemp, each ritual becomes a moment of transformation—not just for the body, but for the soul.

By grounding your mornings, softening your evenings, and celebrating the turning of the seasons with intention, you become a vessel of balance—a living calendar that honors the rhythms of Earth, Moon, Sun, and Self.

Chapter 18: Special Astrological Events and Hemp

Harnessing the Healing Power of Hemp During Eclipses, Retrogrades, and Celestial Shifts

◈ Cosmic Disruption and Earthly Anchoring

Astrological events such as **eclipses, planetary retrogrades, and major transits** act as cosmic punctuation marks—turning points that accelerate personal and collective evolution. These energetic waves often bring emotional upheaval, spiritual breakthroughs, or physical exhaustion. While they can feel chaotic, they are **not here to harm**—they are catalysts for realignment.

During these intensified times, hemp becomes an essential ally. As a plant known for its **grounding, calming, and adaptogenic properties**, hemp can help regulate the nervous system, aid in emotional processing, and assist in ritual practices that support integration rather than overwhelm. Whether you are moving through a disruptive Mercury retrograde or navigating a soul-deep Pluto transit, there is a way to **pair specific CBD products and hemp strains with the archetypal energies** at play.

This chapter will teach you how to anchor yourself with intention, using hemp as a sacred companion through even the most unstable astrological terrain.

◈ Eclipses: Portals of Revelation and Release

◈ What They Are

Eclipses occur when the Sun, Moon, and Earth align in such a way that **shadows are cast and light is temporarily blocked**. Lunar eclipses signal emotional culmination; solar eclipses indicate external reset or rebirth. These events mark **cosmic thresholds** and should be treated with sacred reverence, not casual rituals.

◈ What They Activate

- Sudden realizations
- Endings and beginnings
- Spiritual initiations
- Energetic downloads and release of karmic baggage

◈ **Hemp Pairing Rituals**

Lunar Eclipse (emotional clarity and closure):

- *CBD type:* Full-spectrum with calming terpenes like myrcene or linalool
- *Application:* Use a hemp-infused bath soak under the moon, journal afterward
- *Ritual add-on:* Burn dried hemp leaves mixed with mugwort for divination

Solar Eclipse (reset, new energy):

- *CBD type:* Broad-spectrum or energizing tincture
- *Application:* Drop under the tongue while stating a release intention
- *Ritual add-on:* Use a hemp anointing oil at the solar plexus to activate empowerment

◈ *Avoid high-THC strains during eclipses*, as they may amplify confusion or psychic overwhelm. Instead, stay grounded with hemp and ritual simplicity.

 –

◈ Retrogrades: Revisiting, Realigning, Remembering

◈ What They Are

A retrograde occurs when a planet appears to move backward in the sky. While this is an optical illusion, it symbolizes **a reversal of energy**—inviting us to review, reflect, and sometimes re-experience unresolved patterns.

◈ Common Retrogrades and Their Effects

Planet	Impact	Hemp Support Suggestion
Mercury	Miscommunication, tech issues	CBD teas for anxiety, hemp smokes for clarity
Venus	Relationship shifts, value check	Rose + hemp skin balm, CBD for emotional support
Mars	Aggression, burnout	Cooling CBD salves for muscles, grounding rituals
Jupiter	Philosophical confusion	Herbal CBD tonics with turmeric or fennel
Saturn	Delays, karmic lessons	Hemp root salves, patience-supporting oils
Uranus	Sudden changes, breakthroughs	Fast-acting tinctures + breathwork sessions

Planet	Impact	Hemp Support Suggestion
Neptune	Illusion, fog, dreams	Aromatherapy rituals, sleep blends, lucid tea
Pluto	Transformation, shadow work	Charcoal-infused hemp tinctures or deep meditations

⬦ General Retrograde Hemp Ritual

- Start with a **grounding CBD dose** (preferably full-spectrum)
- Create a quiet ritual space with blue or indigo candlelight
- Reflect on the retrograde's theme in your journal
- Anoint your third eye with **CBD-infused essential oil**
- Close with a mantra such as:

"I am aligned with the wisdom of this review. I grow even in reversal."

◈ Major Transits: Long-Term Energetic Waves

◈ What They Are

Major planetary transits involve outer planets like Jupiter, Saturn, Uranus, Neptune, and Pluto moving through zodiac signs or forming significant aspects (e.g., conjunctions, oppositions, squares) with your **natal chart** or the collective transits. These shifts shape eras—not just days.

◈ What They Impact

- Identity restructuring (e.g., Saturn Return)
- Career and destiny (e.g., Jupiter conjunct Midheaven)
- Psychological death and rebirth (e.g., Pluto transits)
- Collective upheaval or awakening (e.g., Uranus in Taurus)

◈ Suggested Long-Form Hemp Support

Transit Example	Emotional Impact	Hemp Protocol
Saturn Return (Age 28–30, 58–60)	Pressure, maturity, boundaries	Daily CBD capsules + evening reflection rituals
Uranus Opposition (Age ~42)	Sudden rebellion, identity shift	Midday tincture, microdoses for decision-making
Neptune Square (Mid-life fog)	Disillusionment, creativity block	Aromatherapy and dream salves nightly
Pluto Transit to Natal Moon	Emotional purging, trauma rising	Deep healing ceremonies, guided journaling with hemp

◈ Emotional Self-Care & Spiritual Hygiene with Hemp

During heightened astrological events, emotional regulation and energetic hygiene are essential. Here are key hemp practices to maintain balance:

1. CBD Smoke Cleanse

- Use organic hemp flower or pre-roll
- Wave smoke over your body while visualizing disruption dissolving
- Affirm: "I release what does not serve. I root in what remains."

2. Hemp + Sound Bath

- Place CBD oil beneath tongue
- Lie down with binaural beats or planetary frequency soundscapes (e.g., 528Hz for transformation)
- Envision hemp as a frequency conductor guiding cosmic harmonization

3. CBD Anointing for the Chakras

- Solar plexus during solar events
- Heart for Venus retrogrades
- Third eye for Neptune and eclipse season
- Base of spine for Pluto and Saturn transits

◈ Pairing Strains by Cosmic Need

Cosmic Challenge	Ideal Hemp Strain Profile
Emotional overload (eclipses)	High-CBD, indica-dominant, lavender terpenes
Brain fog (Mercury Rx)	CBD + limonene and pinene terpenes for clarity
Relationship tension (Venus Rx)	Rose-enhanced hemp, gentle hybrids
Existential crisis (Pluto transit)	Charcoal-infused full-spectrum tincture, myrcene-rich
Burnout (Saturn or Mars transit)	Cooling hemp balms, CBG blends for stress relief
Intuition sharpening (Neptune transit)	Dream blends with hemp + mugwort or blue lotus

◈ Final Thoughts: Astrology as the Weather, Hemp as the Medicine

Astrology provides the **forecast**—sometimes clear skies, sometimes storms. Hemp provides the **remedy**—whether as a calming tea, a grounding oil, or a ritual ally.

When the cosmos shakes the foundation beneath you, let hemp be the root that holds you steady. Let your rituals be real. Let your healing be daily. And let the stars remind you that **every disruption is an invitation to deepen your alignment.**

Conclusion: Weaving Your Own Cosmic Tapestry

Honoring the Journey of Self-Discovery Through Astrology and Hemp

In a universe governed by rhythm, energy, and intricate design, you are both a participant and a pattern. You are not just reading the stars—you are made of them. You are not merely using hemp—you are remembering the Earth's language through it. What you hold in your hands is not just a book, but an initiation. A re-entry into sacred relationship with yourself, the cosmos above, and the plant kingdom below.

Throughout this guide, you've explored the **twelve zodiac archetypes** and how their energies can be honored, soothed, and amplified with intentional hemp use. You've decoded the roles of the **Sun, Moon, and Ascendant**, followed the **planetary transits** and **lunar tides**, and embraced hemp's power as a botanical ally. You've learned that **ritual is not repetition—it is revelation**. Each use of a tincture, each inhale of calming smoke, each bath infused with CBD and lunar light is a moment of returning to your truth.

But most importantly—you've learned that the journey is *yours* to shape.

◈ The Path Is Not Linear—It Spirals

Like the planets in their orbits, like the Moon in her phases, your path to alignment will move in spirals. There will be seasons of fire, where bold action feels natural. There will be times of retreat, where water invites emotional healing. Astrology is not about becoming something new. It is about **remembering who you already are**, through archetypes that reflect your soul's encoded purpose.

And hemp—this sacred, adaptable, intelligent plant—does not "fix" you. It supports you. It mirrors your needs. It listens to your nervous system and offers grounding, clarity, or softness, depending on what your body and spirit require. It is **not a trend**. It is **a tool of reclamation**—returning your agency over wellness back to your hands, away from disconnection, toward sovereignty.

◈ Create Your Own Rituals

Now that you are fluent in the foundations, you are invited to become a **ritualist of your own life**. There is no single way to blend astrology and hemp. The suggestions and practices you've read are *invitations*, not instructions. As you deepen your understanding of your birth chart and your body, feel free to:

- Design your own **moon rituals** based on your emotional cycles
- Infuse oils or teas based on your **planetary returns**
- Explore strains not only for pain or anxiety—but for **creativity, intimacy, focus, or insight**
- Revisit this text at every **seasonal shift, eclipse, or personal evolution**, building layers of meaning

Your practice will evolve as you do. And that is its power.

◈ A Living Tapestry

Astrology and hemp both honor something mainstream culture often forgets: **you are dynamic, not static**. You are not meant to be the same person in every phase, every cycle, every chapter. Just as the planets shift signs and the hemp plant blooms with variation, your path to balance will take new forms over time.

Let your rituals breathe. Let your understanding deepen. Let your discomfort lead to discovery. Let your doubt be met with gentleness, not judgment. And let the plant teach you how to soften your resistance and open your awareness.

You are weaving your own **cosmic tapestry**—a life woven from light and chlorophyll, stardust and soil, breath and intention. No one else's pattern will look quite like yours. And that is what makes it divine.

◈ Final Blessing

May the Moon's pull guide your intuition.
May the Sun remind you of your power.
May the Earth keep you rooted in calm.
And may hemp be the thread that grounds the stars to your skin.

Welcome to the new age of wellness—where astrology is your map, hemp is your medicine, and *you* are the mystic in motion.

Your journey is only beginning.
Keep looking up.
Keep reaching down.
And above all—**keep aligning**.

Appendix A: Glossary of Astrological Terms

A Clear Guide to the Language of the Stars

Astrology is a symbolic language—rich in archetypes, geometry, and energetic nuance. To fully integrate hemp into your astrological wellness practice, it's essential to understand the key terms that guide celestial interpretation. This glossary offers **accessible, professional definitions** to empower your journey through the heavens and enhance the cosmic connection with your Earth-based rituals.

◈ Core Concepts

Astrology

The study of celestial bodies (like planets and stars) and their symbolic influence on human behavior, natural cycles, and events. Astrology is based on the belief that patterns in the sky reflect patterns on Earth.

Zodiac

A circular band of constellations divided into 12 signs, through which the Sun, Moon, and planets appear to move. Each sign has a unique set of characteristics and governs a 30° segment of the ecliptic (the Sun's apparent path through the sky).

Birth Chart (Natal Chart)

A personal astrological map drawn from the exact time, date, and place of your birth. It shows the positions of planets in zodiac signs and astrological houses, revealing personality traits, challenges, and life path themes.

◈ Planetary Movements

Transit
The current or ongoing movement of planets in the sky in relation to the positions of the planets in your birth chart. Transits reflect evolving life themes and temporary energetic influences.

Retrograde
An apparent backward motion of a planet from Earth's perspective. Retrogrades are symbolic of reviewing, reworking, or revisiting unresolved matters related to the planet's domain (e.g., communication during Mercury retrograde).

Direct Motion
The normal forward motion of a planet across the zodiac, symbolizing progress and external activity in the areas it influences.

◈ Celestial Bodies

The Sun
Represents identity, vitality, ego, and core essence. It's the "self" you are here to become. Rules Leo.

The Moon
Symbolizes emotions, intuition, inner needs, and subconscious patterns. It reflects how you nurture and are nurtured. Rules Cancer.

The Ascendant (Rising Sign)
The zodiac sign rising on the eastern horizon at the moment of birth. It represents your outward behavior, first impressions, and instinctual responses.

The Planets

Each planet symbolizes a psychological function or area of life. Here's a quick guide:

Planet	Represents
Mercury	Communication, thought, learning
Venus	Love, beauty, values, relationships
Mars	Action, desire, aggression, vitality
Jupiter	Expansion, growth, faith, philosophy
Saturn	Discipline, responsibility, structure
Uranus	Innovation, rebellion, awakening
Neptune	Dreams, illusions, spirituality
Pluto	Transformation, power, shadow

◈ Houses and Their Meanings

Houses

The birth chart is divided into 12 segments called "houses," each representing a different area of life. Their meanings include:

House Number	Life Area
1st House	Identity, self-image, appearance
2nd House	Money, values, material possessions
3rd House	Communication, siblings, local travel
4th House	Home, family, emotional foundation
5th House	Creativity, romance, children, joy
6th House	Work, health, daily routines
7th House	Relationships, partnerships, contracts
8th House	Intimacy, transformation, shared resources
9th House	Higher learning, travel, philosophy
10th House	Career, public image, authority
11th House	Friendships, groups, social goals

House Number	Life Area
12th House	Subconscious, endings, solitude, mysticism

◈ Aspects: The Angles Between Planets

Aspects

These are the angular relationships between planets in the chart. Aspects show how planetary energies blend or clash.

Aspect	Degrees Apart	Meaning
Conjunction	0°	Unified energy, intense focus
Sextile	60°	Easy flow, opportunity, cooperation
Square	90°	Tension, challenge, inner conflict
Trine	120°	Harmony, natural talent, ease
Opposition	180°	Polarity, balance, relational dynamics

Each aspect has a unique influence and modifies the tone of the chart. For example, a trine between Venus and Neptune enhances artistic and romantic expression, while a square between Mars and Saturn may indicate inner frustration or hard-earned success.

◇ Astrological Cycles

Lunar Phases

The Moon moves through eight phases every 29.5 days, each with unique energetic qualities:

- **New Moon:** Beginnings, intention setting
- **First Quarter:** Challenges, commitment
- **Full Moon:** Illumination, release, manifestation
- **Last Quarter:** Reflection, rest, closure

Saturn Return

A major life milestone when Saturn returns to the same sign and degree it occupied at your birth (~every 29 years). Often associated with maturity, accountability, and significant life shifts.

Eclipses

Lunar or solar events where the light of the Sun or Moon is obscured. Eclipses reveal truths, provoke change, and mark powerful beginnings or endings.

◈ Interpretive Tools

Chart Ruler

The planet that rules your Ascendant sign. It gives insight into how you move through the world and where your life energy is most concentrated.

Elemental Grouping

Each sign is associated with one of four elements:

- **Fire (Aries, Leo, Sagittarius):** Passion, drive, action
- **Earth (Taurus, Virgo, Capricorn):** Stability, practicality, sensuality
- **Air (Gemini, Libra, Aquarius):** Intellect, communication, ideas
- **Water (Cancer, Scorpio, Pisces):** Emotion, intuition, sensitivity

Modalities

Each sign also has a modality that describes its energetic behavior:

- **Cardinal (Aries, Cancer, Libra, Capricorn):** Initiators, leaders, pioneers
- **Fixed (Taurus, Leo, Scorpio, Aquarius):** Stabilizers, loyal, determined
- **Mutable (Gemini, Virgo, Sagittarius, Pisces):** Adaptable, changeable, flexible

◈ **Integrating with Hemp**

Understanding these terms allows you to apply astrology **with precision and purpose** in your hemp-based wellness practice. Whether you are timing your CBD use with your Saturn return, aligning a hemp bath ritual with the Full Moon in Pisces, or crafting a topical blend based on your 6th house Virgo placement—this glossary empowers you to speak the language of the stars fluently.

Appendix B: Glossary of Hemp Terms

A Practical Guide to Understanding Hemp-Based Wellness

Hemp is a multifaceted plant with therapeutic potential that spans ancient herbal medicine, modern science, and conscious self-care. To fully integrate hemp into your astrological practice, it is essential to understand its components, delivery methods, and biological effects. This glossary provides **clear, accurate definitions** of the most important hemp-related terms, giving you the language and confidence to make informed decisions and design personalized rituals.

◈ Cannabinoids

Cannabinoids

Natural chemical compounds found in hemp and cannabis plants. They interact with the body's endocannabinoid system (ECS) to regulate mood, pain, sleep, immunity, and more. Over 100 cannabinoids have been identified.

CBD (Cannabidiol)

A non-psychoactive cannabinoid known for its calming, anti-inflammatory, and balancing properties. CBD does not produce a "high" and is commonly used for stress relief, anxiety reduction, pain management, and sleep improvement.

THC (Tetrahydrocannabinol)

The main psychoactive cannabinoid found in cannabis that produces euphoria or intoxication. Hemp-derived THC levels must remain below 0.3% by law. While THC can offer pain relief and relaxation, high amounts may cause anxiety or disorientation in sensitive individuals.

CBG (Cannabigerol)

A minor cannabinoid sometimes called the "mother cannabinoid," as it is the precursor to CBD and THC. Known for potential neuroprotective and anti-inflammatory benefits.

CBN (Cannabinol)

A mildly psychoactive cannabinoid often associated with sedative effects. It may support sleep and deep relaxation, particularly when combined with CBD.

◈ The Endocannabinoid System (ECS)

Endocannabinoid System (ECS)
A complex biological system in the human body that maintains home-ostasis (balance). It includes receptors (CB1 and CB2), endocannabi-noids (produced by the body), and enzymes that break down cannabinoids. The ECS influences appetite, mood, memory, immune function, and sleep.

CB1 Receptors
Primarily located in the brain and central nervous system. They regulate mood, emotion, coordination, and pain. THC primarily interacts with CB1 receptors.

CB2 Receptors
Found mostly in the immune system and peripheral tissues. They help regulate inflammation and immune responses. CBD interacts indirectly with CB2 receptors.

◈ Terpenes

Terpenes
Aromatic compounds found in hemp (and all plants) that contribute to its scent and flavor. They also play a therapeutic role by interacting with cannabinoids and enhancing effects—a phenomenon known as the *entourage effect*.

Common Terpenes in Hemp:

Terpene	Aroma/Flavor	Potential Effects
Myrcene	Earthy, musky	Sedation, pain relief, muscle relaxant
Limonene	Citrus	Uplifting, mood-enhancing
Linalool	Floral, lavender	Calming, anti-anxiety
Pinene	Pine	Alertness, anti-inflammatory
Caryophyllene	Spicy, peppery	Anti-inflammatory, stress reduction
Terpinolene	Woody, herbal	Antioxidant, mildly sedative

◈ Delivery Methods

Tincture
A liquid hemp extract (usually oil-based) taken sublingually (under the tongue) for fast absorption into the bloodstream. Often used for systemic relief and daily wellness routines.

Edible
Any hemp-infused food or drink, including gummies, chocolate, tea, or baked goods. Effects take longer to onset (30–90 minutes) but tend to last longer in the body.

Topical
A hemp-based cream, balm, or salve applied directly to the skin. Used for localized relief from muscle aches, inflammation, or skin irritation. Topicals do not enter the bloodstream.

Transdermal Patch
A hemp-infused adhesive patch that delivers cannabinoids through the skin and into the bloodstream over time. Provides consistent dosing and longer-lasting effects.

Smokeable Hemp Flower
Dried hemp buds that can be smoked or vaped. Offers fast-acting relief with a more direct and experiential effect. May contain various terpene profiles.

Inhalation (Vaping)
The use of vaporized hemp oil or flower for rapid cannabinoid delivery via the lungs. Effects are felt quickly but may not last as long as edibles or tinctures.

◈ Hemp Categories & Products

Full-Spectrum CBD

Contains all cannabinoids, terpenes, flavonoids, and trace THC (<0.3%). Promotes the entourage effect and is considered the most holistic option.

Broad-Spectrum CBD

Contains multiple cannabinoids and terpenes but has had all THC removed. Ideal for those sensitive to THC or needing to avoid it for legal or personal reasons.

CBD Isolate

Pure CBD with all other plant compounds removed. Best for individuals who need precision dosing or prefer no other compounds.

Hemp Oil vs. CBD Oil

- **Hemp Oil (Hemp Seed Oil):** Cold-pressed from hemp seeds. Rich in omega-3s and vitamins but contains no cannabinoids. Used for cooking and skincare.
- **CBD Oil:** Extracted from the flowers and leaves of the hemp plant. Contains cannabinoids and therapeutic compounds.

◈ Cultivation and Ethics

Industrial Hemp

A variety of the *Cannabis sativa* plant specifically bred for low THC and high fiber, seed, or CBD content. Legal in many regions and highly sustainable.

Organic Hemp

Hemp grown without pesticides, herbicides, or synthetic fertilizers. Certified organic hemp ensures higher quality and environmental safety.

Sustainable Hemp

Hemp grown using regenerative agricultural practices. Hemp requires minimal water, detoxifies soil, and sequesters carbon—making it one of the most eco-friendly crops.

Third-Party Testing

Independent laboratory testing used to verify product purity, cannabinoid content, and the absence of contaminants (like heavy metals, pesticides, or mold). Always check for a **Certificate of Analysis (COA).**

Bioavailability

The degree and rate at which a cannabinoid is absorbed into the bloodstream. Different methods (edibles, tinctures, vapes) have varying bioavailability.

◈ Ritual and Integration Terms

Hemp Ritual

A sacred or intentional act using hemp for spiritual, emotional, or energetic alignment—such as moon baths, meditation oiling, or seasonal ceremonies.

Entourage Effect

The synergistic interaction between cannabinoids, terpenes, and other compounds in hemp that enhances therapeutic outcomes. Whole-plant use is typically more effective than isolated compounds.

Adaptogen

A natural substance that helps the body adapt to stress and restore balance. Hemp is considered an adaptogen in many herbal traditions due to its regulating effects on the ECS.

◈ Navigating the Plant with Precision

This glossary is designed to empower your confidence and fluency when choosing hemp products for your wellness practice. Whether you're selecting a strain for a retrograde ritual or applying a balm during eclipse season, understanding the terminology deepens your connection to both the **plant and your body**.

Use this appendix as a living reference—highlight, annotate, or create your own entries based on personal experience and intuition.

<u>Message from the Author:</u>

I hope you enjoyed this book, I love astrology and knew there was not a book such as this out on the shelf. I love metaphysical items as well. Please check out my other books:

-Life of Government Benefits

-My life of Hell

-My life with Hydrocephalus

-Red Sky

-World Domination:Woman's rule

-World Domination:Woman's Rule 2: The War

-Life and Banishment of Apophis: book 1

-The Kidney Friendly Diet

-The Ultimate Hemp Cookbook

-Creating a Dispensary(legally)

-Cleanliness throughout life: the importance of showering from childhood to adulthood.

-Strong Roots: The Risks of Overcoddling children

-Hemp Horoscopes: Cosmic Insights and Earthly Healing

- Celestial Hemp Navigating the Zodiac: Through the Green Cosmos

-Astrological Hemp: Aligning The Stars with Earth's Ancient Herb

-The Astrological Guide to Hemp: Stars, Signs, and Sacred Leaves

-Green Growth: Innovative Marketing Strategies for your Hemp Products and Dispensary

-Cosmic Cannabis

-Astrological Munchies

-Henry The Hemp

-Zodiacal Roots: The Astrological Soul Of Hemp

- **Green Constellations: Intersection of Hemp and Zodiac**

-Hemp in The Houses: An astrological Adventure Through The Cannabis Galaxy

-Galactic Ganja Guide

Heavenly Hemp
Zodiac Leaves
Doctor Who Astrology
Cannastrology
Stellar Satvias and Cosmic Indicas
<u>Celestial Cannabis: A Zodiac Journey</u>
AstroHerbology: The Sky and The Soil: Volume 1
AstroHerbology:Celestial Cannabis:Volume 2
Cosmic Cannabis Cultivation
The Starry Guide to Herbal Harmony: Volume 1
The Starry Guide to Herbal Harmony: Cannabis Universe: Volume 2

Yugioh Astrology: Astrological Guide to Deck, Duels and more
Nightmare Mansion: Echoes of The Abyss
Nightmare Mansion 2: Legacy of Shadows
Nightmare Mansion 3: Shadows of the Forgotten
Nightmare Mansion 4: Echoes of the Damned
The Life and Banishment of Apophis: Book 2
Nightmare Mansion: Halls of Despair
<u>Healing with Herb: Cannabis and Hydrocephalus</u>
<u>Planetary Pot: Aligning with Astrological Herbs: Volume 1</u>
Fast Track to Freedom: 30 Days to Financial Independence Using AI, Assets, and Agile Hustles
<u>Cosmic Hemp Pathways</u>
How to Become Financially Free in 30 Days: 10,000 Paths to Prosperity
Zodiacal Herbage: Astrological Insights: Volume 1
Nightmare Mansion: Whispers in the Walls
The Daleks Invade Atlantis
Henry the hemp and Hydrocephalus

10X The Kidney Friendly Diet
Cannabis Universe: Adult coloring book

Hemp Astrology: The Healing Power of the Stars

Zodiacal Herbage: Astrological Insights: Cannabis Universe: Volume 2

<u>Planetary Pot: Aligning with Astrological Herbs: Cannabis Universes: Volume 2</u>

Doctor Who Meets the Replicators and SG-1: The Ultimate Battle for Survival

Nightmare Mansion: Curse of the Blood Moon

<u>The Celestial Stoner: A Guide to the Zodiac</u>

Cosmic Pleasures: Sex Toy Astrology for Every Sign

Hydrocephalus Astrology: Navigating the Stars and Healing Waters

Lapis and the Mischievous Chocolate Bar

Celestial Positions: Sexual Astrology for Every Sign

Apophis's Shadow Work Journal: : A Journey of Self-Discovery and Healing

Kinky Cosmos: Sexual Kink Astrology for Every Sign

Digital Cosmos: The Astrological Digimon Compendium

Stellar Seeds: The Cosmic Guide to Growing with Astrology

Apophis's Daily Gratitude Journal

Cat Astrology: Feline Mysteries of the Cosmos

The Cosmic Kama Sutra: An Astrological Guide to Sexual Positions

Unleash Your Potential: A Guided Journal Powered by AI Insights

Whispers of the Enchanted Grove

Cosmic Pleasures: An Astrological Guide to Sexual Kinks

369, 12 Manifestation Journal

Whisper of the nocturne journal(blank journal for writing or drawing)

The Boogey Book

Locked In Reflection: A Chastity Journey Through Locktober

Generating Wealth Quickly:How to Generate $100,000 in 24 Hours

Star Magic: Harness the Power of the Universe

The Flatulence Chronicles: A Fart Journal for Self-Discovery

The Doctor and The Death Moth

Seize the Day: A Personal Seizure Tracking Journal

The Ultimate Boogeyman Safari: A Journey into the Boogie World and Beyond

Whispers of Samhain: 1,000 Spells of Love, Luck, and Lunar Magic: Samhain Spell Book

Apophis's guides:Witch's Spellbook Crafting Guide for Halloween

<u>Frost & Flame: The Enchanted Yule Grimoire of 1000 Winter Spells</u>

<u>The Ultimate Boogey Goo Guide & Spooky Activities for Halloween Fun</u>

Harmony of the Scales: A Libra's Spellcraft for Balance and Beauty

The Enchanted Advent: 36 Days of Christmas Wonders

Nightmare Mansion: The Labyrinth of Screams

Harvest of Enchantment: 1,000 Spells of Gratitude, Love, and Fortune for Thanksgiving

The Boogey Chronicles: A Journal of Nightly Encounters and Shadowy Secrets

The 12 Days of Financial Freedom: A Step-by-Step Christmas Countdown to Transform Your Finances

Sigil of the Eternal Spiral Blank Journal

A Christmas Feast: Timeless Recipes for Every Meal

Holiday Stress-Free Solutions: A Survival Guide to Thriving During the Festive Season

Yu-Gi-Oh! Holiday Gifting Mastery: The Ultimate Guide for Fans and Newcomers Alike

Holiday Harmony: A Hydrocephalus Survival Guide for the Festive Season

Celestial Craft: The Witch's Almanac for 2025 – A Cosmic Guide to Manifestations, Moons, and Mystical Events

Doctor Who: The Toymaker's Winter Wonderland

Tulsa King Unveiled: A Thrilling Guide to Stallone's Mafia Masterpiece

Pendulum Craft: A Complete Guide to Crafting and Using Personalized Divination Tools

Nightmare Mansion: Santa's Eternal Eve

Starlight Noel: A Cosmic Journey through Christmas Mysteries

The Dark Architect: Unlocking the Blueprint of Existence

Surviving the Embrace: The Ultimate Guide to Encounters with The Hugging Molly

The Enchanted Codex: Secrets of the Craft for Witches, Wiccans, and Pagans

Harvest of Gratitude: A Complete Thanksgiving Guide

Yuletide Essentials: A Complete Guide to an Authentic and Magical Christmas

Celestial Smokes: A Cosmic Guide to Cigars and Astrology

Living in Balance: A Comprehensive Survival Guide to Thriving with Diabetes Insipidus

Cosmic Symbiosis: The Venom Zodiac Chronicles

The Cursed Paw of Ambition

Cosmic Symbiosis: The Astrological Venom Journal

Celestial Wonders Unfold: A Stargazer's Guide to the Cosmos (2024-2029)

The Ultimate Black Friday Prepper's Guide: Mastering Shopping Strategies and Savings

Cosmic Sales: The Astrological Guide to Black Friday Shopping

Legends of the Corn Mother and Other Harvest Myths

Whispers of the Harvest: The Corn Mother's Journal

The Evergreen Spellbook

The Doctor Meets the Boogeyman

The White Witch of Rose Hall's SpellBook

The Gingerbread Golem's Shadow: A Study in Sweet Darkness

The Gingerbread Golem Codex: An Academic Exploration of Sweet Myths

The Gingerbread Golem Grimoire: Sweet Magicks and Spells for the Festive Witch

The Curse of the Gingerbread Golem

10-minute Christmas Crafts for kids

<u>Christmas Crisis Solutions: The Ultimate Last-Minute Survival Guide</u>

Gingerbread Golem Recipes: Holiday Treats with a Magical Twist

The Infinite Key: Unlocking Mystical Secrets of the Ages

Enchanted Yule: A Wiccan and Pagan Guide to a Magical and Memorable Season

Dinosaurs of Power: Unlocking Ancient Magick

Astro-Dinos: The Cosmic Guide to Prehistoric Wisdom

Gallifrey's Yule Logs: A Festive Doctor Who Cookbook

The Dino Grimoire: Secrets of Prehistoric Magick

The Gift They Never Knew They Needed

The Gingerbread Golem's Culinary Alchemy: Enchanting Recipes for a Sweetly Dark Feast

A Time Lord Christmas: Holiday Adventures with the Doctor

Krampusproofing Your Home: Defensive Strategies for Yule

Silent Frights: A Collection of Christmas Creepypastas to Chill Your Bones

Santa Raptor's Jolly Carnage: A Dino-Claus Christmas Tale

Prehistoric Palettes: A Dino Wicca Coloring Journey

The Christmas Wishkeeper Chronicles

The Starlight Sleigh: A Holiday Journey

Elf Secrets: The True Magic of the North Pole

Candy Cane Conjurations

Cooking with Kids: Recipes Under 20 Minutes

Doctor Who: The TARDIS Confiscation

The Anxiety First Aid Kit: Quick Tools to Calm Your Mind

Frosty Whispers: A Winter's Tale

The Infinite Key: Unlocking the Secrets to Prosperity, Resilience, and Purpose

The Grasping Void: Why You'll Regret This Purchase

Astrology for Busy Bees: Star Signs Simplified

The Instant Focus Formula: Cut Through the Noise

The Secret Language of Colors: Unlocking the Emotional Codes

Sacred Fossil Chronicles: Blank Journal

The Christmas Cottage Miracle

Feeding Frenzy: Graboid-Inspired Recipes

Manifest in Minutes: The Quick Law of Attraction Guide

The Symbiote Chronicles: Doctor Who's Venomous Journey

Think Tiny, Grow Big: The Minimalist Mindset

The Energy Key: Unlocking Limitless Motivation

New Year, New Magic: Manifesting Your Best Year Yet

Unstoppable You: Mastering Confidence in Minutes

Infinite Energy: The Secret to Never Feeling Drained

Lightning Focus: Mastering the Art of Productivity in a Distracted World

Saturnalia Manifestation Magick: A Guide to Unlocking Abundance During the Solstice

Graboids and Garland: The Ultimate Tremors-Themed Christmas Guide

12 Nights of Holiday Magic

The Power of Pause: 60-Second Mindfulness Practices

The Quick Reset: How to Reclaim Your Life After Burnout

The Shadow Eater: A Tale of Despair and Survival

The Micro-Mastery Method: Transform Your Skills in Just Minutes a Day

Reclaiming Time: How to Live More by Doing Less

Chronovore: The Eternal Nexus

The Mind Reset: Unlocking Your Inner Peace in a Chaotic World
Confidence Code: Building Unshakable Self-Belief
Baby the Vampire Terrier
Baby the Vampire Terrier's Christmas Adventure
Celestial Streams: The Content Creator's Astrology Manual
The Wealth Whisperer: Unlocking Abundance with Everyday Actions
The Energy Equation: Maximize Your Output Without Burning Out
The Happiness Algorithm: Science-Backed Steps to Joyful Living
Stress-Free Success: Achieving Goals Without Anxiety
Mindful Wealth: The New Blueprint for Financial Freedom
The Festive Flavors of New Year: A Culinary Celebration
The Master's Gambit: Keys of Eternal Power
Shadowed Secrets: Groundhog Day Mysteries
Beneath the Burrow: Lessons from the Groundhog
Spring's Whispers: The Groundhog's Prediction
The Limitless Mindset: Unlock Your Untapped Potential
The Focus Funnel: How to Cut Through Chaos and Get Results
Bold Moves: Building Courage to Live on Your Terms
The Daily Shift: Simple Practices for Lasting Transformation
The Quarter-Life Reset: Thriving in Your 20s and 30s
The Art of Shadowplay: Building Your Own Personal Myth
The Eternal Loop: Finding Purpose in Repetition
Burrowing Wisdom: Life Lessons from the Groundhog
Shadow Work: A Groundhog Day Perspective
Love in Bloom: 5-Minute Romantic Gestures
The Shadowspell Codex: Secrets of Forbidden Magick
The Burnout Cure: Finding Balance in a Busy World
The Groundhog Prophecy: Unlocking Seasonal Secrets
Nog Tales: The Spirited History of Eggnog
Six More Weeks: Embracing Seasonal Transitions
The Lumivian Chronicles: Fragments of the Fifth Dimension

Money on Your Mind: A Beginner's Guide to Wealth
The Focus Fix: Breaking Through Distraction
January's Spirit Keepers: Mystical Protectors of the Cold
Creativity Unchained: Unlocking Your Wildest Ideas in 2025
Manifestation Mastery: 365 Days to Rewrite Your Reality
The Groundhog's Mirror: Reflecting on Change
The Weeping Angels' Christmas Curse
Burrowed in Time: A Groundhog Day Journey
Heartbeats: Poems to Share with Your Valentine
Dino Wicca: The Sacred Grimoire of Prehistoric Magick
Courage of the Pride: Finding Your Inner Roar
The Lion's Leap: Bold Moves for Big Results
Healthy Hustle: Achieving Without Overworking
Practical Manifesting: Turning Dreams into Reality in 2025
Jurassic Pharaohs: Unlocking the Magick of Ancient Egypt and Dino Wicca
The Happiness Equation: Small Changes for Big Joy
The Confidence Compass: Finding Your Inner Strength
Whispers in the Hollow: Tales of the Forgotten Beasts
Echoes from the Hollow: The Return of Forgotten Beasts
The Hollow Ascendant: The Rise of the Forgotten Beasts
The Relationship Reset: Building Better Connections
Mastering the Morning: How to Win the Day Before 8 AM
The Shadow's Dance: Groundhog Day Symbolism
Cupid's Kitchen: Quick Valentine's Day Recipes
Valentine's Day on a Budget: Love Without Breaking the Bank
Astrocraft: Aligning the Stars in the World of Minecraft
Forecasting Life: Groundhog Day Reflections
Bleeding Hearts: Twisted Tales of Valentine's Terror
Herbal Smoke Revolution: The Ultimate Guide to Nature's Cigarette Alternative
Winter's Wrath: The Complete Survival Blueprint for Extreme Freezes.

The Groundhog's Shadow: A Tale of Seasons
Burrowed Insights: Wisdom from the Groundhog
Sensual Strings: The Art of Erotic Bondage
Whispered Flames: Unlocking the Power of Fire Play
Forgotten Shadows: A Guide to Cryptids Lost to Time
Six Weeks of Secrets: Groundhog Day's Hidden Messages
Shadows and Cycles: Groundhog Day Reflections
The Art of Love Letters: Crafting the Perfect Message
Romantic Getaways at Home: Turning Your Space into Paradise
Purrfect Brews: A Cat Lover's Guide to Coffee and Companionship
The Groundhog's Wisdom: Timeless Lessons for Modern Life
The Shadow Oracle: Groundhog Day as a Predictor
Emerging from the Burrow: A Journey of Renewal
The Language of Love: Learning Your Partner's Love Style
Authorpreneur: The Ultimate Blueprint for Writing, Publishing, and Thriving as an Author
Weathering the Seasons: Groundhog Day Perspectives
Valentine's Day Magic: A Guide to Romantic Rituals
The Shadow Chronicles: Stories of Groundhog Day
Love and Laughter: Fun Games for Valentine's Day
AstroRealty: Unlocking the Stars for Property Success
The Groundhog's Path: A Guide to Seasonal Balance
Groundhog Day Diaries: Reflections in the Shadow
The Groundhog's Light: Illuminating the Path Ahead
Valentine's Traditions from Around the World
AI Wealth Revolution: Unlocking the Trillionaire Mindset
Love Rekindled: Reigniting Passion in Relationships
Single and Thriving: Self-Love on Valentine's Day
Emerald Legends: Mystical Tales of Ireland
Green Alchemy: Harnessing Nature's Magic
The Hearts of Horror: A Valentine's Day Nightmare

The Leprechaun's Guide to Wealth and Wisdom

Dancing with the Sidhe: Celebrating the Otherworld

Shamrocks and Shadows: Mysteries of the Green Isle

Emerald Energy: Harnessing Luck and Growth

The Gingerbread Golem's Valentine: A Sweetheart's Guide to Love and Enchantment

The Celtic Knot: Weaving Life and Destiny

Green Fire: Elemental Magic for St. Patrick's Day

Clover Chronicles: Finding Your Inner Luck

Ireland's Mystical Creatures: A Field Guide

Gingerbread Golem's Love Almanac

Prowl and Thrive: The Lion's Guide to Success

Love Alchemy: Transforming Your Life Through Heart Energy

WORLD DOMINATION: Woman's Rule 3:The New Life

The Midnight Rose: A Guide to Lunar Love Spells

The Forbidden Letters: Writing Your Own Love Prophecy

Luck and Lore: St. Patrick's Day for Modern Mystics

The Green Path: A Pagan Celebration of Renewal

The Dark Architect's Guide to Reprogramming Reality

Prankster's Paradise: A Guide to Harmless Hijinks

Manifest Your Reality: The Law of Attraction Simplified

The TARDIS Owner's Manual: Understanding the Doctor's Ship: *A complete guide to the TARDIS, its technology, secrets, and mysteries*

Starlit Romance: Astrology Secrets for Finding True Love

The Time Lord's Atlas: A Complete Guide to the Whoniverse: *A breakdown of the locations, planets, and dimensions explored in Doctor Who*

Sweetheart Shadows: The Dark Side of Love and Attraction

February Fire: Reigniting Passion in Every Area of Life

The Self-Love Toolkit: 5 Ways to Embrace Who You Are

February Sparks: Ignite Your Dreams in 28 Days

March to Success: A 31-Day Action Blueprint
Ancient Paths: The 13 Sacred Principles of Dino Wicca
Echoes of Tomorrow: Navigating the AI Revolution
The Wellness Blueprint: Balancing Mind, Body, and Soul
Green Horizons: Sustainable Living for a Better Tomorrow
The AI Wealth Code: How to Make Millions with Automation
AI-Powered Creativity: Writing, Art, and Music for Profit
Extinction Rites: Rebirthing Your Soul Through Prehistoric Magick
Sacred Serpents tarot
Celestial Enchantment blank journal
Star Strains
Culinary Journeys: Exploring Global Flavors at Home
The Hollowvale Curse
The Hollowvale Harvest
The Egg of Transformation: Awakening Your Inner Power
Blooming Into Power: A Wiccan Guide to Spring Awakening
The Nightmare Nexus: The Third Doctor's Perilous Haunting
Digital Detox: Reclaiming Your Life in a Connected World
Ostara's Path: Walking the Spiral of Renewal
The Sacred Hare
Financial Freedom: Building Wealth in the Modern Age
Spring's Cauldron: Stirring the Waters of Change
The Hollowvale Pact
Quantum Consciousness: The Science of Reality Shifting
The Hollowvale Hunger
The Sacred Waters Within: A Witch's Guide to Hydrocephalus Magick
The Raven's Nest: Building a Life of Unshakable Stability
AI and the Human Mind: The Future of Intelligence
The Hollowvale Reckoning
Timeless Love: Building and Maintaining Lasting Relationships

The Raven's Roar: Unlocking Unstoppable Confidence

Raven Sight: Awakening Intuition and Inner Wisdom

The Butterfly Effect: Small Changes, Big Transformations

Taming the Boogeyman: How to Conquer Your Inner Fears

The Magick of Green: Awakening Earth's Energy in You

The Entrepreneurial Mindset: Secrets to Business Success

The Hollowvale End

The Shadow Luck Ritual: Reclaiming Power from Your Dark Side

Spring Magick for Beginners: A Simple Guide to Seasonal Energy Work

Doctor Who: The Hollowvale Conundrum

The March of Miracles: Unlocking Synchronicities in Spring

Unveiling the Cosmos: A Guide to Stargazing and Space Exploration

The Ultimate Guide to Surviving an Economic Collapse

The AI Gold Rush: How to Profit from the AI Revolution

Bastet's Shadow: The Hidden Power of Feline Magick

The Bastet Codex: Unlocking the Goddess's Magickal Secrets

Purring Spells: Harnessing Bastet's Healing Frequencies

Bastet's Nine Lives: Rebirth, Transformation, and Immortality Spells

Primal Currents: Hydrocephalus Magick in the Path of Dino Wicca

The Digital Gold Rush: Mastering E-Commerce and Online Sales

Future Shock: Adapting to the Next Decade of Change

The Quantum Mindset: Think Like a Billionaire

Sacred Motherhood: Awakening the Divine Feminine Within

The Mother's Spellbook: Enchantments for Love, Protection, and Prosperity

The Witch's Guide to Parenting: Raising Empowered and Intuitive Children

The Magick of Motherhood: Reclaiming Your Power Through Rituals

The Pagan Path to Self-Love: A Goddess's Guide to Worth and Confidence

Wild Woman Magick: Unleashing Your Primal Power

The Money Magnet Blueprint: Unlocking Unlimited Wealth

Biohacking 101: Unlock Your Body's Full Potential

The Wild Father: A Pagan Guide to Strength and Wisdom

The Sacred Masculine: Unlocking Your Inner Power

The Druid's Compass

The Warrior's Mindset

The Father's Fire

Odin's Path

Ancestral Bonds

The House That Whispers

The Magician's Code

The Wild Hunt

The Green Man's Path

The Altar of Success

The Shadow and the Sword

The High Priestess's Guide to Energy Healing

The Lunar Mother

The Sacred Self-Care Grimoire

The Womb Wisdom Codex

The Wheel of the Mother

The Witch's Guide to Manifestation

The Q2 Reset

The Ultimate Guide to AI-Powered Passive Income

Escape the 9-5

AI Feline Fortunes

The Tear-Stained Grimoire

Razorblade Runes

Cemetery Sirens

The Midnight Wristwatch
The Town That Forgets
AI Horror & Creepypasta
The Hollow Frequency
The Breach Echo
The Quiet Between Worlds
The Sigil of Tharan-Khul
Summon the Vault of Y'ha'ten
The Becoming Codex
The Profit of Az'ra-nar
The Drowned Logos
Echoes of the Eldritch Will
The Deep Ledger
Necronomicon of Networth
Covenant of the Wealthwyrm
The Whisperer's Manifesto
The Rites of Azh-K'luth
The Ark of the Crawling Coin
The Tithe of Shadows
Inkheart Abyss
The Timewinds of Y'ha-nthlei
The Spiral Labyrinth of Azag-Nirrh
The Gallifreyan Heresy of the Black Pharaoh
The Psalms of Nyog-Sotha
Black Rain Alchemy
The Infinite Maw
The Entropic Blueprint
The Oracle of Sh'guul
The Book of Breach
The Drowned Saint's Testament
Dreamcraft of the Sleeper God
The Silence Market
Cthonomics: The Dark Wealth Algorithm

Invocation of the Ten-Eyed King
Wealthbound to the Wyrm Below
Become the Unnameable
Codex of the Sovereign Flame
Rituals of Relentless Becoming
The Shadow Ascends
The Eyes Beneath You
The Will That Wakes Worlds
Silence Is a Weapon
The Mirror That Screams
The Whisper Between Moments
The Mind That Devours Fear
The Myth of the Finished Self
The Architect of Your Madness
The Voice You've Buried
The Discipline of Madness
Stormborn: Awakening Your Inner Tempest
The Mind That Ate Time
Unbind Your Becoming
The Pact You Owe Yourself
The Devourer's Diet
The Acid That Carves the Path
The Tower You Must Burn
The Breath Between Worlds
Speak Like the Deep
The Labyrinth Within
The Spine of the Sea God
Rejection Is a Portal
The Crown You Refused
The Scar Is the Spell
The Lightless Flame
The Habit of Becoming Horrific
ChickenJockey Chaos

The Gatekeeper Within

You Are Not Your Name

The Compass of the Mad

The Archive of Unsent Letters

What the Mirror Can't Show You

The Knife You Needed

Worship Nothing, Become Everything

The Other Voice

The Body the World Forgot

The Vein of the Void

The Black Bone Codex

The Puzzle of the Hidden Self (Millennium Puzzle)

The Eye That Sees the Lie *(Millennium Eye)*

The Ring of Return (Millennium Ring)

The Rod of Relentless Will *(Millennium Rod)*

The Tally of the Soul (Millennium Tauk/Necklace)

The Key to the Locked Timeline (Millennium Key)

The Scale of Sacred Decisions (Millennium Scales)

Inferno Bites: The UnOfficial Minecraft Lava Cookbook

Rot in the Attic

Prana: The Hidden Force of Your Infinite Self

The Shadow Realm Within: Transforming Darkness Into Destiny

The Borderland Collapse

Claws of Protection: Bastet's Defensive Magick

Mr. Ring-a-Ding's Madness

Yugioh Astrology: Celestial Deckcraft and Duel Destiny (2026–2027 Edition)

The Seal You Signed: Unlocking the Power You Once Feared

The Puzzle of Infinite Minds: Unlocking the Mentalism Hidden Within

The Eye That Mirrors the All: Secrets of Inner Reflection

Doctor Who: The Toymaker's Broadcast

Rootwake: The Carbon Covenant

Skitter Logic: Unlearning the Fear That Built You

Doctor Who: The World That Froths

Rootwake: The Fizz That Rewrites Flesh

Rootwake: Frothfather of the World

The Holly Pact: Blood Beneath the Mistletoe

The 2nd Mass Principle: Building Unbreakable Tribes

Web of Wits: A Survival Guide to Encounters with Anasi the Spider (Aunt Nancy)

The Hexbreaking Handbook: Effective Spells to Remove Curses

Pop Alchemy: Transform Your Life One Sip at a Time

The Mason Code: Leading in Unleadable Times

Petosiris and the Fifth Chamber of Thoth

The Ether Seed Within

The Parent of Tomorrow

Petosiris's Pyramid of Perpetual Wealth

Unlearn the World

Grimoire of the Hollow Tongue

Zodiac Weeds: Finding Your Strain Through the Stars

Aquarius Rises in the Bank

The Sugar God's Smile

The Skinclock Reversal: Biohacking the Face of Time

Debtburn: How to Obliterate What You Owe Forever

The Ice Cream Oracle: What Your Cone Says About Your Future

Silence Is Sovereignty: The Power of Being Unreadable

The Wind That Whispers Through Stone

Get Some Tarot cards: https://www.makeplayingcards.com/sell/apophis-occult-shop

Get   some   shirts: https://www.bonfire.com/store/apophis-shirt-emporium/

<u>**Instagrams:**</u>
@apophis_enterprises,
@apophisbookemporium,
@apophisscardshop
Twitter: @apophisenterpr1
 Tiktok:@apophisenterprise
Youtube: @sg1fan23477
Hive: @sg1fan23477
CheeLee: @SG1fan23477

Podcast: Apophis Chat Zone: https://open.spotify.com/show/
5zXbrCLEV2xzCp8ybrfHsk?si=fb4d4fdbdce44dec

Newsletter: https://apophiss-newsletter-27c897.beehiiv.com/

If you want to support me or see posts of other projects that I have come over to: **buymeacoffee.com/mpetchinskg**
I post there daily several times a day

Get your Dinowicca or Christmas themed digital products, especially Santa Raptor songs and other musics. Here: **https://sg1fan23477.gumroad.com**

Apophis Yuletide Digital has not only digital Christmas items, but it will have all things with Dinowicca as well as other Digital products.